DEDALO AGENCY

COSTA RICA

Travel guide

HOW TO PLAN
A TRIP TO COSTA RICA
WITH BEST TIPS
FOR FIRST-TIMERS

Edited by: Domenico Russo and Francesco Umbria
Design e layout: Giorgia Ragona
Book series: Journey Joy

COSTA RICA

Travel guide

Index

Introduction

Welcome to Costa Rica, a land where the vibrant spirit of "pura vida" meets the breathtaking beauty of nature. This Central American paradise offers a blend of lush jungles, serene beaches, and majestic volcanic landscapes that inspire awe and wonder. As you embark on your journey through Costa Rica, this guide will be your trusted companion, providing not just directions and suggestions but a gateway to truly experiencing the essence of this remarkable country.

Costa Rica, nestled between the Pacific Ocean and the Caribbean Sea, is a haven for biodiversity. Its rainforests teem with life, from colorful toucans and playful monkeys to the elusive jaguar. The country's commitment to conservation is evident in its numerous national parks and protected areas, making it a model for eco-tourism worldwide. Each corner of Costa Rica offers unique landscapes and adventures, from the misty cloud forests of Monteverde to the volcanic hot springs of Arenal.

Your journey will begin in the vibrant capital, San José, a city rich in culture and history. Here, you can explore historic theaters, dive into gold and jade museums, and savor the flavors of the culinary district, Barrio Escalante. Moving on to the natural wonders of Arenal Volcano and La Fortuna, you'll discover the thrill of zip-lining through the canopy, the relaxation of soaking in natural hot springs, and the awe of hiking around one of the country's most iconic volcanoes.

In the cloud forests of Monteverde, you'll be immersed in an ethereal world where biodiversity thrives. Sky-high adventures await you, from hanging bridges to coffee and chocolate tours. Guanacaste and the Nicoya Peninsula will greet you with sun-kissed beaches, perfect waves for surfing, and untouched natural beauty. Manuel Antonio National Park offers a blend of pristine beaches and rich wildlife, ensuring you experience the best of both worlds.

The remote Osa Peninsula and Corcovado National Park will take you into the wild heart of Costa Rica, where biodiversity is at its peak. The Caribbean Coast introduces a different vibe with its vibrant culture and natural beauty, from the tranquility of Tortuguero to the lively streets of Puerto Viejo. Costa Rican cuisine will delight your palate with its rich flavors, whether you're indulging in street food or fine dining.

Traveling on a budget in Costa Rica is not only possible but also rewarding. This guide offers tips on how to enjoy the best of Costa Rica without overspending. Our top picks for cultural experiences will immerse you in the local way of life, from coffee plantation tours to participating in turtle release programs. And for those considering a longer stay, we've got extended itinerary options to ensure every moment is packed with discovery.

As you explore Costa Rica, you'll find that it's not just a destination but a way of life. The warmth of its people, the richness of its culture, and the stunning beauty of its landscapes will leave a lasting impression. Whether you're drawn by the call of the wild, the promise of adventure, or the simple joy of living "pura vida," Costa Rica welcomes you with open arms.

So, let's embark on this journey together. Welcome to Costa Rica, where every moment is an adventure, and every experience is a story waiting to be told.

COSTA RICA TRAVEL GUIDE

CHAPTER 1:
San José
················

San José, the vibrant heart of Costa Rica, is where the journey into the rich tapestry of Costa Rican culture, history, and modern life begins. As the bustling capital city nestled in the Central Valley, surrounded by lush mountains and volcanic peaks, San José is a melting pot of traditions and contemporary lifestyles. Here, the essence of Pura Vida—a term that encapsulates the local approach to life, emphasizing happiness and well-being—permeates through the colorful streets, markets, and the warm smiles of its people.

Despite being often overlooked in favor of the country's famed natural landscapes, San José is a treasure trove of cultural experiences waiting to be discovered. From its historic theaters and museums to the lively markets and parks, the city offers a unique blend of experiences that connect visitors with the soul of Costa Rica. Walking through San José, you'll encounter a dynamic urban canvas, where historic architecture stands side by side with modern street art, telling the story of a city that's constantly evolving yet firmly rooted in its heritage.

As we delve into the heart of San José, we invite you to explore its key landmarks, each with its own story and significance to the city's cultural and historical landscape. Let this chapter be your guide to discovering the charm of San José, a city where every corner offers a new discovery and every experience brings you closer to understanding the true spirit of Costa Rica.

National Theatre of Costa Rica

The National Theatre of Costa Rica (Teatro Nacional de Costa Rica), standing with dignity in the heart of San José, is not just an architectural masterpiece but the cultural epicenter of the nation. Opened in 1897, this opulent neoclassical building is a symbol of Costa Rica's artistic aspirations and a testament to its commitment to cultural preservation. The theater's lavish interiors, adorned with intricate murals and elegant furnishings, host some of the country's most significant cultural performances, from operas to symphonies.

Visitors are encouraged to take a guided tour of the theater to fully appreciate its architectural beauty and historical significance. And if time permits, attending a live performance here is an unforgettable experience that connects you with the artistic soul of Costa Rica. Even when the curtains are closed, the theater's café offers a chance to enjoy a cup of Costa Rican coffee in a setting that transports you back to the splendor of the late 19th century.

Gold Museum (Museo del Oro)

Beneath the Plaza de la Cultura lies a dazzling world of pre-Columbian treasures at the Gold Museum (Museo del Oro). This underground museum houses one of the largest collections of gold artifacts in the Americas, showcasing the intricate craftsmanship and the complex societal structures of Costa Rica's indigenous populations. The artifacts, ranging from delicate jewelry to symbolic animal figurines, offer a window into the lives and beliefs of the people who lived in this region long before the arrival of Europeans.

Exploring the Gold Museum is a journey through time, revealing the sophistication and the spiritual depth of the ancient cultures of Costa Rica. The museum also features a numismatic collection and temporary exhibitions that delve into various aspects of Costa Rican history and culture. For a deeper understanding of the significance of these artifacts, audio guides are available in multiple languages, providing context and stories that bring the ancient world to life.

Central Market (Mercado Central)

No visit to San José would be complete without a stroll through the Central Market (Mercado Central), the pulsating heart of the city's daily life. Established in 1880, this bustling labyrinth of vendors offers an authentic glimpse into the Costa Rican way of life. Here, you can find everything from exotic fruits and vegetables to traditional handicrafts, herbs, and souvenirs.

The Central Market is also a culinary haven, where you can sample traditional Costa Rican dishes like gallo pinto, casado, and the irresistible chicharrones. Grab a seat at one of the small sodas (local eateries) within the market and savor the flavors that define Costa Rican cuisine. It's not just a place for shopping; it's an experience that engages all your senses, from the colorful sights and sounds to the delicious aromas and tastes that fill the air.

La Sabana Metropolitan Park

La Sabana Metropolitan Park, often referred to as "the lungs of San José," is the city's largest and most important urban park. Stretching over 72 hectares, this verdant oasis amidst the urban sprawl is a favorite among locals and tourists alike for leisure and recreation. Once an international airport, La Sabana has been transformed into a vibrant space filled with lakes, sports fields, jogging paths, and areas for picnics and relaxation. It's a testament to San José's commitment to providing green spaces and promoting a healthy lifestyle among its residents.

The park is not just for recreation; it's also a cultural hub, home to the Costa Rican Art Museum, housed in the old airport terminal building. As you stroll through La Sabana, you'll notice various outdoor sculptures and artworks, further enhancing its appeal as a place of culture and relaxation. It's a perfect spot to unwind after exploring the bustling city, offering a tranquil setting for a leisurely walk or a morning jog amidst the lush foliage and serene ponds.

Visitors to La Sabana Metropolitan Park can enjoy its amenities free of charge, making it an ideal location for budget-conscious travelers. The park is open daily from dawn until dusk, offering a safe and peaceful environment throughout the day. For those interested in sports, several courts and fields can be rented for a small fee. Weekends are particularly lively, as families and groups of friends gather to enjoy the open space, so for a quieter experience, consider visiting on a weekday morning. Don't forget to bring sunscreen and plenty of water, as the open areas can get quite sunny during the day.

Museum of Costa Rican Art

The Museum of Costa Rican Art, nestled within the eastern edge of La Sabana Park, is a cultural gem dedicated to preserving and showcasing the nation's artistic heritage. Housed in the building that once served as the country's first international airport terminal, the museum boasts an impressive collection of Costa Rican art from the mid-19th century to the present. The range of artworks, including paintings, sculptures, and prints, offers a comprehensive overview of the country's artistic evolution and highlights the creativity and diversity of Costa Rican artists.

The museum's architecture is a piece of art in itself, with its neoclassical design and the beautifully preserved murals that adorn its walls. Among the most notable features is the mural in the Golden Room (Salón Dorado), which depicts various aspects of Costa Rican life and history. This mural is considered a national treasure and is a must-see for visitors.

Admission to the Museum of Costa Rican Art is free, making it an accessible cultural experience for everyone. The museum is open from Tuesday to Sunday, and guided tours are available upon request, offering insights into the artworks and the history of the building. The best time to visit is in the morning when the museum is less crowded, allowing for a more intimate viewing experience. Photography is allowed, so don't hesitate to capture the beauty of the artworks and the historic building for your memories.

Jade Museum (Museo del Jade)

Located in the heart of San José, the Jade Museum (Museo del Jade) is an extraordinary facility dedicated to preserving and exhibiting the largest collection of pre-Columbian jade artifacts in the world. The museum, operated by the National Insurance Institute (INS), showcases more than 7,000 pieces of jade, alongside ceramic, gold, and stone objects that offer a glimpse into the lives of the indigenous peoples of Costa Rica before the arrival of Europeans. The jade artifacts, ranging from intricate jewelry to symbolic figures and ceremonial items, highlight the skill and artistry of these ancient cultures.

The modern, five-story building of the Jade Museum provides visitors with a state-of-the-art museum experience, featuring interactive exhibits and displays that not only focus on the significance of jade in the social and economic systems of pre-Columbian societies but also explore the geology of jade and the technology behind its carving. The museum's layout guides visitors through a journey of discovery, from the ground floor with its broad overview of Costa Rican history to the upper floors dedicated to thematic exhibits on jade and other materials.

The Jade Museum is open to the public from Monday to Sunday, with a small admission fee that supports the museum's conservation and educational programs. It's recommended to allocate at least two hours for your visit to fully appreciate the depth and breadth of the collection. Early morning or late afternoon visits are advisable to avoid the crowds, especially during the peak tourist season. Guided tours are available in multiple languages, providing valuable insights into the exhibits and enhancing your museum experience. Remember to check the museum's official website or contact them directly for the most current information on opening hours, ticket prices, and special exhibitions.

Barrio Escalante (Culinary District)

Barrio Escalante, once a residential neighborhood, has blossomed into San José's premier culinary district, a vibrant testament to the city's burgeoning food scene. This trendy area is a food lover's paradise, lined with a diverse array of eateries, cafes, and bars, each offering a unique twist on local and international cuisines. From traditional Costa Rican dishes to innovative fusion food, the culinary offerings in Barrio Escalante cater to all palates and preferences.

Strolling through the streets of Barrio Escalante, you'll encounter the heart and soul of Costa Rica's culinary innovation. The district's relaxed atmosphere, combined with its architectural charm, makes for a delightful dining experience. Food festivals and culinary events are common here, offering visitors a chance to dive deep into the local food culture.

For the best experience, consider visiting Barrio Escalante in the evening when the area comes alive with locals and travelers alike. Many restaurants and cafes offer outdoor seating, perfect for enjoying the cool Costa Rican evenings. Reservations are recommended for the more popular spots, especially on weekends. Don't miss the opportunity to try a craft beer from one of the local microbreweries, a growing trend in Costa Rica's culinary scene.

San José by Night

As the sun sets, San José transforms, offering a different vibe and a new world of experiences. The city's nightlife is as diverse as its culture, ranging from lively bars and nightclubs to cultural performances and live music venues. Whether you're looking to dance the night away, enjoy a quiet drink with friends, or catch a live performance, San José's nighttime scene has something for everyone.

One of the highlights of San José by night is its live music scene, featuring genres from traditional Latin rhythms to contemporary international music. Jazz cafes and salsa clubs are particularly popular, offering visitors a chance to experience the joy and passion of Costa Rican music and dance.

Safety is an important consideration when exploring any city at night, and San José is no exception. Stick to well-lit, busier streets and consider using a reputable taxi service or ride-sharing app to get around. Most nightlife venues are welcoming and safe, but it's always wise to be aware of your surroundings and keep personal belongings secure.

Day Trip to Poás Volcano

A day trip to Poás Volcano National Park offers an unforgettable escape into the natural beauty that surrounds San José. Just an hour's drive from the city, this active volcano is one of Costa Rica's natural wonders, featuring one of the largest accessible craters in the world. The park offers a variety of trails, leading visitors through cloud forests to breathtaking viewpoints overlooking the crater and its turquoise sulfuric lake.

Visiting Poás Volcano requires some planning. The park limits the number of visitors each day to minimize environmental impact, so booking your ticket in advance is essential. Early morning visits are recommended, as the clouds tend to roll in later in the day, obscuring the view of the crater. Be sure to bring layers, as the altitude can make it significantly cooler than in San José.

Final Thoughts

San José, with its rich cultural tapestry, vibrant culinary scene, and proximity to natural wonders, offers travelers a unique blend of experiences. While exploring the city, take the opportunity to venture beyond the guidebook recommendations. Visit local markets, engage with the city's street art scene, and chat with locals to get a deeper sense of San José's identity. The city's public transport system, including buses and taxis, is an efficient way to navigate, but walking is often the best way to experience the city's hidden gems.

For those interested in sustainable tourism, San José offers various eco-friendly activities and initiatives, aligning with Costa Rica's commitment to conservation and sustainable living. Exploring the city's green spaces, supporting local artisans, and choosing eco-conscious accommodations are just a few ways to make your visit more sustainable.

San José serves as the perfect starting point for exploring Costa Rica's diverse landscapes and cultures. Whether you're drawn to its urban charm or the call of the wild beyond, San José promises an adventure that's as enriching as it is exhilarating. Remember, the essence of Pura Vida isn't just found in the destinations you visit but in the moments you experience and the memories you create.

COSTA RICA TRAVEL GUIDE

CHAPTER 2:
Arenal Volcano and La Fortuna

The region surrounding Arenal Volcano and the town of La Fortuna is a showcase of the raw, natural beauty that Costa Rica is celebrated for worldwide. This area combines the dramatic landscape of an active volcano with lush rainforests, hot springs, and a myriad of outdoor adventures, making it an essential stop for any traveler to Costa Rica. La Fortuna, named after its fortuitous escape from the eruptions of the Arenal Volcano, serves as the gateway to exploring the natural wonders of this vibrant region.

The juxtaposition of the imposing Arenal Volcano against the backdrop of verdant forests and crystal-clear waters creates a scene of unparalleled beauty. Here, the synergy between the natural world and sustainable tourism practices offers visitors a unique opportunity to immerse themselves in Costa Rica's biodiversity while ensuring the preservation of this magnificent landscape for future generations.

As we delve into the heart of Arenal and La Fortuna, prepare to be captivated by the sights, sounds, and experiences that await. From thrilling zipline tours through the canopy to tranquil moments in nature-infused hot springs, this chapter will guide you through the best that Arenal and La Fortuna have to offer, providing practical tips to enhance your adventure in one of Costa Rica's most iconic regions.

Arenal Volcano National Park

Arenal Volcano National Park is a testament to the awe-inspiring power of nature. The park is centered around the Arenal Volcano, a perfect conical volcano that dominated the landscape until its last eruption cycle ended in 2010. Despite its current dormancy, the volcano remains a magnificent sight, with its lush slopes offering a habitat for a rich variety of wildlife, including howler monkeys, sloths, and numerous bird species. The park's network of trails allows visitors to explore the diverse ecosystems at the volcano's base, from secondary rainforest to the remnants of lava flows.

For the best experience, the Arenal Volcano National Park offers several guided tours that provide not only the safety of navigating the terrain but also the knowledge of local guides who can point out the subtle wonders of the ecosystem. The early morning or late afternoon is the ideal time to visit when the wildlife is most active and the heat and crowds are less intense.

Admission to the park comes with a fee, which contributes to its maintenance and conservation efforts. It's advisable to wear sturdy hiking shoes and bring rain gear, as the weather can change rapidly. Also, don't forget to pack water and snacks for the journey, as the park's natural beauty deserves a full day's exploration.

La Fortuna Waterfall

Descending 70 meters into a lush rainforest, La Fortuna Waterfall is a breathtaking natural wonder that captures the essence of Costa Rica's wild beauty. The waterfall, easily accessible from the town of La Fortuna, cascades into a crystalline pool that invites a refreshing swim in the midst of the tropical greenery. The journey to the waterfall involves a hike down a staircase of over 500 steps, offering multiple vantage points to admire the falls and the surrounding rainforest.

Visiting La Fortuna Waterfall is a must-do for nature lovers and photographers alike, with the mist from the falls creating a magical atmosphere that's almost ethereal. The site is well-equipped with facilities, including restrooms and changing areas, making it a comfortable excursion for all visitors.

There's an entrance fee to access the waterfall, which helps fund local conservation efforts. To avoid the busiest times and enjoy a more serene experience, consider visiting early in the morning. After your swim or photo session, take the time to explore the nearby trails, which offer opportunities to spot wildlife and enjoy the tranquility of the rainforest. Water shoes are recommended for navigating the rocky pool area, and remember to bring a waterproof camera to capture the beauty of this iconic Costa Rican landmark.

Hot Springs

The natural hot springs around Arenal Volcano are one of the area's most indulgent attractions, offering a perfect blend of relaxation and natural beauty. Heated by the geothermal activity of the volcano, these thermal waters are rich in minerals and believed to have therapeutic properties. The surrounding lush landscapes and the backdrop of the volcano create an idyllic setting for unwinding after a day of adventure. Many resorts and spas around La Fortuna offer access to private hot springs, each with its unique charm, from cascading waterfall pools to serene, forest-shrouded basins.

For those seeking a more secluded experience, public hot springs provide a budget-friendly alternative without sacrificing the magical experience of soaking in warm, mineral-rich waters amidst the rainforest. Whether you choose the luxurious amenities of a resort or the natural simplicity of the public springs, an evening in Arenal's hot springs is an experience not to be missed.

To make the most of your visit, consider staying at a resort that offers unlimited access to their hot springs. If visiting public springs, aim for early morning or late evening when the crowds thin out, and the experience becomes more intimate. Remember to stay hydrated, especially if you plan to spend significant time in the hot springs, and bring a waterproof case for your phone or camera to capture the serene beauty of these thermal waters.

Hanging Bridges

The hanging bridges in the Arenal region offer an unparalleled opportunity to experience the rainforest canopy up close. Suspended high above the forest floor, these bridges provide a unique vantage point from which to observe the rich biodiversity of the area, including a variety of birds, plants, and possibly even some of the forest's more elusive inhabitants, such as monkeys and sloths. The network of bridges, part of several private reserves near Arenal Volcano, allows for safe and accessible exploration of this complex ecosystem, making it an ideal activity for nature lovers and families alike.

Walking across the hanging bridges is an adventure in itself, with each step offering new sights, sounds, and the thrill of being suspended in the air. Guided tours are available and recommended, as they enhance the experience by providing insights into the flora and fauna that inhabit the rainforest canopy.

To visit the hanging bridges, consider booking a guided tour which often includes transportation from La Fortuna. Wear comfortable walking shoes and bring rain gear, as the weather can be unpredictable. Early morning is the best time to visit for wildlife viewing and to avoid the afternoon crowds. Check with your tour provider or the reserve for the most current information on admission fees and opening hours.

Canopy Tours and Zip Lining

Canopy tours and zip-lining are among the most thrilling ways to experience the lush landscapes of the Arenal region. These activities offer an adrenaline-pumping journey through the treetops, providing breathtaking views of the surrounding rainforest and the Arenal Volcano. With a variety of courses available, ranging from family-friendly to extreme adventure, there's an option to suit every thrill-seeker's level of comfort and experience.

Safety is a top priority, with experienced guides and state-of-the-art equipment ensuring a secure yet exhilarating adventure. Beyond the thrill, zip-lining gives you a bird's-eye view of the rainforest's biodiversity, gliding over rivers, canyons, and through the dense canopy, all while possibly spotting wildlife in their natural habitat.

When planning a canopy tour or zip-lining adventure, book with a reputable company that prioritizes safety and environmental respect. Wear comfortable clothing that can get a bit dirty, closed-toe shoes, and consider bringing a strap for your glasses or sunglasses. Most tours offer lockers or safe places to store your belongings during your adventure. Morning tours typically offer clearer skies and cooler temperatures, making for an ideal zip-lining experience. Remember, these activities are popular, so booking in advance is recommended, especially during peak travel seasons.

Lake Arenal

Lake Arenal, a vast man-made reservoir at the base of the Arenal Volcano, plays a significant role in Costa Rica's energy production but is equally renowned for its natural beauty and array of outdoor activities. The lake's serene waters reflect the imposing silhouette of the volcano, creating a stunning landscape that's perfect for photography, especially at sunrise or sunset. Kayaking, windsurfing, fishing, and stand-up paddleboarding are popular on Lake Arenal, offering visitors unique ways to explore the scenic surroundings.

The area around Lake Arenal is also known for its abundant wildlife, including a variety of birds, making it a favorite spot for bird watchers. The surrounding forests and pastures contribute to the lake's serene and picturesque setting, inviting visitors to relax and immerse themselves in nature.

For those interested in water sports, several local operators offer equipment rentals and guided tours. Early morning is the best time for activities like kayaking and paddleboarding when the water is calmest and the wildlife is most active. If you're driving around the lake, there are several spots to stop and enjoy the view, but be mindful of the weather as it can change quickly. A visit to Lake Arenal can be easily combined with a trip to the hot springs or a hike in the Arenal Volcano National Park for a full day of exploration.

Arenal by Night

Exploring Arenal by night offers a completely different perspective on the region's natural beauty, with night tours available for those interested in witnessing the nocturnal activities of the rainforest's inhabitants. Guided night walks through the forest reserves around Arenal allow visitors to see and hear the rainforest come alive with the sounds of frogs, insects, and nocturnal birds, under the guidance of knowledgeable local guides who can point out the creatures that only emerge after dark.

For a more relaxing nighttime experience, consider visiting one of the many hot springs resorts that offer evening access. Soaking in the warm, mineral-rich waters under a starry sky, with the silhouette of the Arenal Volcano in the distance, is an unforgettable way to end a day of adventure.

Night tours in the rainforest require advance booking, and it's advisable to wear long pants, long-sleeved shirts, and sturdy walking shoes to protect against insects and the terrain. Bringing a flashlight or headlamp can also enhance your experience, although many tour operators will provide them. As for the hot springs, nighttime is often less crowded, making it an ideal time for a more serene and intimate experience. Check with the hot springs resorts for special evening rates and packages that may include dinner or other amenities.

Day Trip to Río Celeste

A day trip to Río Celeste, located in Tenorio Volcano National Park, is a must-do for those visiting the Arenal region. The river's striking turquoise color, a result of the volcanic minerals mixing with the water, creates a surreal and captivating landscape. The hike to Río Celeste leads visitors through lush rainforest to the river's famous waterfall, an ethereal blue cascade that is a highlight of the trail. Along the way, hikers can also see the river's "teñideros," where the water turns its distinctive color, and enjoy the park's rich biodiversity.

The hike to Río Celeste is considered moderate, suitable for visitors with a reasonable level of fitness. It's important to wear comfortable hiking shoes as the trail can be muddy and slippery, especially after rain. Bringing a change of clothes is also recommended, as you might get wet during the hike.

The best time to visit Río Celeste is during the dry season, from December to April, when the trails are more accessible and the river's color is at its most vibrant. Entry to Tenorio Volcano National Park is subject to an admission fee, and the park is open from 8:00 AM to 4:00 PM, but it's advisable to start your hike early in the morning to avoid the crowds and to ensure you have enough time to enjoy the trail and return before the park closes. Guided tours are available and recommended for those interested in learning more about the park's ecology and history.

Arenal Cuisine

The Arenal region, with its rich volcanic soil and abundant rainfall, is a fertile ground for producing a wide variety of fruits, vegetables, and other ingredients that make up the local cuisine. Dining in Arenal offers an authentic taste of Costa Rican flavors, with a focus on fresh, locally sourced produce. Restaurants and sodas (local eateries) in La Fortuna and around Lake Arenal serve traditional dishes such as "casado" – a hearty meal consisting of rice, beans, salad, plantains, and a choice of meat or fish – and "ceviche", a fresh seafood dish marinated in citrus juices.

For those looking to experience the full breadth of Arenal cuisine, many local farms and plantations offer tours that include tastings of coffee, chocolate, and other local specialties. These tours not only provide insight into the agricultural practices of the region but also allow visitors to sample the freshest flavors right from the source.

To truly immerse yourself in the culinary landscape of Arenal, consider visiting during the harvest season for coffee (November to January) or cacao (September to December), when many farms offer special tours and tastings. Dining at local sodas is not only a way to enjoy authentic Costa Rican dishes but also supports the local economy. Don't forget to ask your hosts or local residents for their restaurant recommendations, as they often know the best spots for traditional fare that might not be on the typical tourist radar.

Final Thoughts

Exploring Arenal Volcano and La Fortuna offers an unparalleled adventure into the heart of Costa Rica's natural beauty, combining thrilling outdoor activities with the tranquility of hot springs and the richness of local culture and cuisine. As you plan your visit, remember that the key to a truly memorable experience lies in embracing the Pura Vida lifestyle, taking the time to connect with both the landscape and the local communities.

For those seeking to make the most of their time in Arenal, combining activities like hiking in the national park in the morning with relaxing in a hot spring in the evening can offer a balanced and fulfilling day. Additionally, considering eco-friendly and sustainable travel options helps ensure the preservation of this beautiful region for future generations. Local guides and tour operators not only provide valuable insights and access to hidden gems but also contribute to the local economy.

Lastly, while Arenal's natural wonders are a major draw, the region's culture and cuisine offer deep insights into Costa Rican life. Participating in a local cooking class, visiting a farmers' market, or simply engaging with residents can enrich your travel experience beyond the usual tourist activities. As you depart from Arenal, carry with you not only photos and souvenirs but also stories and experiences that reflect the true essence of Costa Rica.

CHAPTER 3:
Monteverde Cloud Forest Reserve

Monteverde Cloud Forest Reserve is a jewel in the crown of Costa Rica's ecological attractions, renowned for its breathtaking biodiversity, mysterious cloud-covered forests, and its pioneering role in conservation and sustainable tourism. This unique ecosystem, perched high in the mountains of the Cordillera de Tilarán, is home to thousands of species of plants, birds, insects, and mammals, some of which are found nowhere else on earth.

The area around Monteverde, including the quaint town of Santa Elena, offers a blend of natural wonders and cultural experiences, making it a must-visit destination for nature lovers and eco-tourists alike.

Visiting Monteverde is not just about exploring the cloud forest; it's about immersing yourself in a community that has embraced sustainability and conservation as a way of life. The area's rich biodiversity is matched by the cultural diversity of its residents, including Quakers who settled here in the 1950s and played a significant role in the area's conservation efforts. Whether you're hiking through the cloud forest, enjoying the local cuisine, or learning about sustainable practices, Monteverde offers a profound connection to nature and an inspiring example of environmental stewardship.

As you prepare to explore Monteverde, remember that the elevation and the cloud cover can make the weather cooler and wetter than in other parts of Costa Rica. Packing layers and waterproof gear will ensure you're comfortable and dry as you embark on your adventures in this enchanting cloud forest.

Cloud Forest Exploration

The heart of the Monteverde experience is, without doubt, the exploration of its famous cloud forest. The Monteverde Cloud Forest Reserve offers a network of trails that weave through the lush, verdant landscape, shrouded in mist and alive with the sounds of nature. This ethereal environment is home to an astonishing array of flora and fauna, including the resplendent quetzal, orchids in myriad colors, and the rare and elusive jaguar. Guided walks, both day and night, are available and highly recommended to enhance your understanding and appreciation of the forest's complex ecosystem.

Exploring the cloud forest requires patience and quiet; the dense foliage and mist can make wildlife spotting challenging, but the rewards are unparalleled. The canopy is teeming with life, from swinging monkeys to gliding birds, while the forest floor is a mosaic of ferns, mosses, and orchids.

For the best experience, book a guided tour early in the morning when animals are most active and the forest is less crowded. Be sure to wear comfortable, waterproof hiking boots and bring binoculars for bird watching. The reserve charges an entrance fee, which is used to support conservation and education efforts in Monteverde. Check the reserve's official website or contact them directly for the most current information on opening hours and guided tour options.

Sky Adventures Monteverde Park

Sky Adventures Monteverde Park offers a thrilling way to experience the beauty of the cloud forest from above. The park's aerial tram glides gently over the canopy, offering panoramic views of the forest and the opportunity to spot wildlife from a unique perspective. For those seeking more adrenaline, the park's zip lines provide an exhilarating ride through the tree-tops, with one of the longest zip lines in the country.

The park also features hanging bridges that allow visitors to walk among the canopy, offering a closer look at the biodiversity of the cloud forest. These bridges are an excellent opportunity for photography and bird watching, providing a bird's-eye view of the forest's intricate layers.

Advance booking for Sky Adventures Monteverde Park is recommended, especially for zip-lining and guided tours on the hanging bridges. Wear comfortable clothing and sturdy shoes, and consider bringing a light rain jacket, as the weather can change quickly. The park has different packages and tickets for its attractions, so review the options to choose the best fit for your interests and schedule. Whether you're gliding above the canopy or walking amongst the treetops, Sky Adventures offers a memorable and unique way to connect with the natural beauty of Monteverde.

Coffee and Chocolate Tours

Monteverde's fertile lands and cool climate offer the perfect conditions for growing coffee and cacao, two of Costa Rica's most beloved exports. Coffee and chocolate tours in the area provide a fascinating insight into the journey of these products from seed to cup and bean to bar, respectively. Visitors have the opportunity to learn about the meticulous processes involved in cultivation, harvesting, and processing, all while surrounded by the beautiful scenery of Monteverde's farms.

The tours are not only educational but also interactive, allowing participants to get hands-on experience with the coffee and chocolate-making processes. Tasting sessions are a highlight, where you can sample the rich flavors and subtle differences between various batches, all produced using sustainable farming practices that respect the local ecosystem.

For the best experience, book your tour in advance, especially during peak tourist seasons. Most tours last between 2 to 3 hours and are offered in both English and Spanish. Wearing comfortable shoes is recommended, as you'll be walking through the farms. These tours are a fantastic way to support local businesses and learn more about Costa Rica's commitment to sustainable agriculture. Don't forget to purchase some coffee or chocolate directly from the farms to take a piece of Monteverde home with you.

The Monteverde Butterfly Gardens

The Monteverde Butterfly Gardens, or Mariposario, is a must-visit for nature lovers, offering a closer look at Costa Rica's incredible butterfly diversity. This enchanting attraction houses several greenhouses, each mimicking different habitats to support a variety of butterfly species. Knowledgeable guides lead visitors through the gardens, sharing fascinating facts about butterfly biology, behavior, and conservation efforts in the region. Besides butterflies, the gardens also provide a habitat for other insects and arachnids, highlighted in the insect museum. This part of the tour offers insights into the vital roles these creatures play in the ecosystem, promoting a greater appreciation for even the smallest inhabitants of the cloud forest.

The Monteverde Butterfly Gardens are open daily, and guided tours are available throughout the day. The best time to visit is on sunny mornings when butterflies are most active. Be sure to bring your camera, as the gardens offer numerous opportunities for up-close photography with these colorful insects. Admission fees are reasonable and contribute to the maintenance of the gardens and the educational programs they offer.

Hummingbird Gallery

Adjacent to the entrance of the Monteverde Cloud Forest Reserve, the Hummingbird Gallery is a delightful spot where visitors can observe and photograph a variety of hummingbird species flitting about in a natural garden setting. Feeders attract these vibrant birds, providing guests with the chance to see them up close. The gallery is not only a place to admire hummingbirds but also serves as an educational resource, with information about the different species and their significance to the ecosystem.

The intimate setting allows for a peaceful interaction with nature, making it a perfect stop before or after exploring the cloud forest. The gallery also features a gift shop with handcrafted goods and souvenirs, many of which are made by local artisans, offering another opportunity to support the community.

There's no admission fee for the Hummingbird Gallery, making it an accessible activity for all visitors. The best times to visit are early in the morning or late in the afternoon when the birds are most active. While photography is encouraged, it's recommended to turn off the flash to avoid startling the birds. Whether you're an avid birdwatcher or simply looking for a tranquil spot to enjoy Monteverde's natural beauty, the Hummingbird Gallery is a charming addition to your itinerary.

Monteverde by Night

Experiencing Monteverde by night is a unique adventure that unveils the nocturnal side of the cloud forest, a world seldom seen by the day-tripping visitor. Night tours in Monteverde offer an intimate glimpse into the lives of the forest's after-dark inhabitants, including nocturnal birds, insects, amphibians, and mammals like sloths and kinkajous. Guided by expert naturalists, these tours are a thrilling way to explore the forest's hidden depths, where every rustle and chirp adds to the night's mystique. The darkness amplifies the senses, making the experience of walking through the forest at night unforgettable. The guides are adept at spotting the creatures that lurk in the shadows, providing fascinating insights into their behaviors and roles within the ecosystem. It's a chance to see the forest in a new light, or rather, in the new darkness, which reveals the true vibrancy of Monteverde's biodiversity.

To participate in a night tour, it's best to book in advance, especially during the high season. Wear warm clothing, as the temperature can drop significantly after sunset, and sturdy shoes for walking on uneven terrain. Most tours provide flashlights, but bringing your own headlamp can free up your hands for balance and photography. These tours typically start just after dusk, making it possible to enjoy an early dinner in Santa Elena before embarking on your nocturnal expedition.

Day Trip to Santa Elena Cloud Forest Reserve

A day trip to Santa Elena Cloud Forest Reserve offers a different perspective on the cloud forest ecosystem, complementing the experience of visiting the Monteverde Reserve. Santa Elena is less crowded, allowing for a more tranquil exploration of the lush, mossy forests that are home to a vast array of flora and fauna. The reserve is managed by a local community organization, with proceeds supporting conservation and education within the community.

Trails in Santa Elena wind through dense forest and offer stunning views of the Arenal Volcano on clear days. The reserve also features a canopy tower, providing visitors with the opportunity to ascend above the treetops for panoramic views of the surrounding forest and beyond. It's a haven for birdwatchers, with chances to spot many of the species endemic to the cloud forest.

The Santa Elena Cloud Forest Reserve is open daily, and an entrance fee is required. Arriving early in the morning not only maximizes your chances of wildlife sightings but also offers the tranquility of having the trails more to yourself. Guided tours are available and recommended for those interested in learning more about the unique ecosystem. Be sure to check the weather and dress appropriately, as the conditions can change quickly. Waterproof clothing, comfortable walking shoes, and layers are advisable for the variable Monteverde climate.

Sustainable Tourism and Conservation Efforts in Monteverde

Monteverde is a global example of how sustainable tourism can support conservation efforts and community development. The region's approach to eco-tourism emphasizes minimizing the impact on the environment while maximizing the benefits to the local community and visitors. Conservation organizations, along with private reserves and local businesses, work together to protect the area's biodiversity through research, education, and sustainable practices.

Visitors to Monteverde can contribute to these efforts in several ways, from choosing to stay in eco-friendly accommodations to participating in educational tours that highlight the importance of conservation. Many local businesses and tour operators are certified for their sustainable practices, ensuring that your travel dollars support those who are committed to preserving Monteverde's natural and cultural heritage.

To engage in sustainable tourism in Monteverde, consider using refillable water bottles, supporting local artisans by purchasing locally made souvenirs, and respecting wildlife and trail rules during your hikes. Additionally, volunteering opportunities and donations to conservation projects offer more direct ways to contribute to Monteverde's environmental preservation. By traveling responsibly, you help ensure that Monteverde remains a vibrant, lush, and welcoming destination for generations to come.

Monteverde Cuisine

Monteverde's unique climate and fertile lands contribute to a diverse agricultural landscape, which is reflected in its rich and varied cuisine. The area is particularly renowned for its dairy products, with local cheese factories producing some of the finest cheeses in Costa Rica. Monteverde also offers a plethora of dining options that range from traditional Costa Rican dishes to international cuisine, all prepared with fresh, locally sourced ingredients. The region's coffee and chocolate are not to be missed, with several cafes and restaurants highlighting these products in their menus.

For those keen to dive into the local flavors, typical dishes such as "gallo pinto" (a rice and beans mixture) for breakfast, "casado" (a combination plate usually featuring rice, beans, salad, plantain, and a protein) for lunch, and fresh trout, a local specialty, offer a taste of the traditional Costa Rican diet. Vegetarian and vegan visitors will find Monteverde to be quite accommodating, with many eateries offering plant-based options.

To fully experience Monteverde cuisine, consider visiting a local farmer's market to sample and purchase fresh produce, including exotic fruits and vegetables you might not find elsewhere. Dining at small, family-owned sodas is not only a way to enjoy authentic meals but also supports the local economy. Don't forget to ask for a cup of locally grown coffee to complement your meal, ensuring a truly Monteverde dining experience.

Final Thoughts

As your journey through Monteverde comes to a close, remember that the essence of this enchanting region extends far beyond the cloud forests and into the heart of its community and sustainable practices. Monteverde exemplifies how nature and humanity can coexist harmoniously, with conservation at the forefront of its ethos. To make the most of your visit, consider engaging with the community through cultural exchanges, be it a cooking class, a visit to a local school, or a community-led tour, which can offer deeper insights into the local way of life.

While Monteverde's main attractions are undoubtedly its natural wonders, taking time to appreciate the subtler aspects of the area can enrich your experience. The misty mornings, the chorus of nocturnal creatures, and the warmth of the local people all contribute to the magic of Monteverde.

Lastly, as an eco-conscious traveler, you play a vital role in preserving the beauty and integrity of Monteverde for future visitors. Practicing leave-no-trace principles, opting for sustainable tour operators, and respecting wildlife guidelines are just a few ways you can contribute positively to this unique ecosystem. Monteverde is more than just a destination; it's a testament to the beauty of nature and the power of conservation, offering lessons and experiences that will stay with you long after you've returned home.

COSTA RICA TRAVEL GUIDE

CHAPTER 4:
Guanacaste and the Nicoya Peninsula
···

Guanacaste and the Nicoya Peninsula are celebrated for their sun-drenched beaches, sprawling national parks, and a laid-back vibe that encapsulates Costa Rica's Pura Vida lifestyle. This region, with its dry tropical climate and diverse ecosystems, offers a stark contrast to the misty cloud forests of Monteverde, showcasing the country's ecological variety. Guanacaste's coastline is a haven for surfers, sun-seekers, and nature enthusiasts, while the Nicoya Peninsula, accessible yet remote, provides a sanctuary for those looking to escape the hustle and bustle of daily life.

The area's cultural heritage, influenced by Chorotega indigenous traditions and Spanish colonial history, adds another layer of richness to the visitor's experience. Guanacaste is not just about the stunning landscapes; it's a place where you can immerse yourself in Costa Rican culture, from traditional music and dance to local cuisine.

Exploring Guanacaste and the Nicoya Peninsula offers a blend of adventure and relaxation. Whether you're surfing the perfect wave, discovering hidden beaches, or simply soaking up the sunsets that light up the Pacific horizon, this region promises unforgettable experiences. Remember to respect the natural environments and local communities as you enjoy all that Guanacaste has to offer, ensuring that this paradise remains pristine for generations to come.

Tamarindo Beach

Tamarindo Beach, with its golden sands and crystal-clear waters, is the epitome of a tropical paradise and one of the most popular destinations in Guanacaste. Renowned for its excellent surfing conditions, Tamarindo attracts wave riders from around the globe, yet its appeal extends far beyond the surf. The beach is also a fantastic spot for families, sunbathers, and anyone looking to enjoy water sports, including snorkeling, kayaking, and stand-up paddleboarding.

The town of Tamarindo has developed significantly in response to its popularity, offering a wide range of accommodations, restaurants, and shops. Despite its growth, Tamarindo maintains a laid-back atmosphere, with beachfront bars and cafes providing the perfect setting to unwind after a day in the sun.

For the best surfing conditions, visit Tamarindo during the dry season (December to April). If you're new to surfing, numerous surf schools offer lessons for all ages and skill levels. To fully enjoy Tamarindo's natural beauty, consider staying at one of the eco-friendly resorts or lodges that emphasize sustainability. While in the area, don't miss the chance to explore the Tamarindo Wildlife Refuge, where you can experience the area's rich biodiversity on a guided kayak tour through the mangroves.

Santa Rosa National Park

Santa Rosa National Park stands as a monument to Costa Rica's rich history and biodiversity. Established in 1971 to protect the site of the 1856 Battle of Santa Rosa, the park now also conserves one of the last remnants of dry tropical forest in the world. Within its boundaries, visitors can explore a variety of ecosystems, from mangrove wetlands to savannah and marine areas, which are home to an impressive array of wildlife, including deer, monkeys, and hundreds of bird species.

The park offers several hiking trails that lead to historical sites, pristine beaches, and lookout points with spectacular views of the Pacific. One of the park's highlights is the La Casona Museum, which details the history of the battle and the importance of conservation efforts in Guanacaste.

To visit Santa Rosa National Park, an entrance fee is required, which contributes to the conservation and maintenance of the park. The best time to visit is during the dry season when the trails are most accessible. Given the park's size and the diversity of attractions, consider hiring a local guide to make the most of your visit. Be sure to bring plenty of water, sunscreen, and insect repellent, and wear appropriate footwear for hiking. Santa Rosa's remote beaches are also nesting sites for several species of sea turtles, offering opportunities for responsible wildlife watching, especially at night.

Nosara and Yoga Retreats

Nosara, nestled along the Nicoya Peninsula's stunning Pacific coastline, has carved out a niche as a tranquil haven for yoga enthusiasts and those seeking wellness and spiritual rejuvenation. With its pristine beaches, lush jungles, and a strong emphasis on conservation and wellness, Nosara provides the perfect backdrop for a transformative yoga experience. The town is home to numerous yoga studios and retreat centers, offering classes and workshops for all levels, from beginners to advanced practitioners.

The integrative approach to wellness in Nosara extends beyond yoga; many retreats also offer meditation sessions, spa treatments, and organic cuisine, promoting a holistic lifestyle that harmonizes body, mind, and spirit. The community's commitment to environmental sustainability is reflected in the eco-friendly practices of local businesses, making Nosara an ideal destination for eco-conscious travelers.

When planning a yoga retreat in Nosara, consider the timing of your visit and the type of experience you're looking for. The dry season (December to April) offers sunny days ideal for beach yoga and outdoor activities, while the green season (May to November) brings lush landscapes and quieter settings for introspection. Many retreats fill up quickly, so booking in advance is recommended. Don't forget to explore Nosara's natural beauty, from its renowned surf spots to protected wildlife areas, enhancing your wellness journey with the healing power of nature.

Montezuma Waterfall

The Montezuma Waterfall, a breathtaking cascade located near the quaint town of Montezuma on the Nicoya Peninsula, is one of Costa Rica's hidden gems. This spectacular natural attraction is composed of three separate falls, with the largest plunging over 24 meters into a crystal-clear pool below. A favorite among adventurous travelers and locals alike, the falls offer an idyllic spot for swimming, cliff jumping, and soaking up the surrounding natural beauty.

Reaching the Montezuma Waterfall involves a hike through lush forest terrain, which adds to the adventure and allure of visiting this site. The path to the waterfall allows visitors to immerse themselves in the area's vibrant flora and fauna, with opportunities to spot wildlife along the way.

To visit the Montezuma Waterfall, wear comfortable, sturdy footwear suitable for hiking and bring a swimsuit if you plan to take a dip in the pools. While the first waterfall is easily accessible, reaching the upper falls requires a bit more effort and caution. Local guides are available for hire and can enhance your experience by providing insights into the area's ecology and ensuring your safety during the hike. There is no entrance fee to visit the waterfall, but donations are welcome to support local conservation efforts. The best time to visit is in the morning when the site is less crowded, offering a more peaceful experience.

Surfing in Malpaís and Santa Teresa

The twin coastal towns of Malpaís and Santa Teresa, located on the Nicoya Peninsula's southwestern tip, have emerged as premier destinations for surfers from around the globe. Renowned for their consistent surf, these towns attract a mix of beginners looking to catch their first wave and seasoned surfers seeking challenging breaks. The laid-back atmosphere, stunning sunsets, and vibrant surf culture make Malpaís and Santa Teresa not just surf destinations but lifestyle choices for many who visit.

The beaches offer a variety of surf spots suitable for different skill levels, with surf schools and rental shops readily available to provide lessons and gear. Beyond surfing, Malpaís and Santa Teresa boast a growing community of artists, yogis, and chefs, contributing to a rich cultural scene that complements the surfing lifestyle.

For the best surf conditions, visit during the dry season when offshore winds create ideal waves. However, the green season offers its own charm, with fewer crowds and lush landscapes. Whether you're a novice or an experienced surfer, consider taking a lesson from a local surf school to get insider tips on the best spots and techniques. Respect the local surf etiquette, protect the environment by using reef-safe sunscreen, and immerse yourself in the Pura Vida spirit that defines the surfing community in Malpaís and Santa Teresa.

Guanacaste by Night

Guanacaste transforms as the sun sets, offering a vibrant nightlife that caters to a variety of tastes and preferences. From the lively beach bars of Tamarindo to the more laid-back lounges in Nosara and Santa Teresa, the region provides ample opportunities for visitors to enjoy live music, dance, and mingle with both locals and travelers. Many establishments host regular events, including live bands and DJ sets, showcasing local and international talent. For those seeking a more serene evening, a night walk on the beach under the stars offers a tranquil and romantic experience.

In addition to bars and clubs, night markets and cultural events are often held in the larger towns, offering a glimpse into Guanacaste's local arts, crafts, and culinary delights. These events are a great way to experience the local culture and support artisans and small business owners.

When exploring Guanacaste's nightlife, it's important to stay safe. Stick to well-lit areas and consider traveling in groups or with a companion. Check with your accommodation for recommendations on the best places to go and any areas to avoid. Remember that while Guanacaste is generally safe, it's always wise to exercise common sense, especially at night. Using licensed taxis or rideshare services when getting around at night is recommended, ensuring a fun and safe experience in Guanacaste after dark.

Boat Tours and Snorkeling

The crystal-clear waters and rich marine life of Guanacaste and the Nicoya Peninsula make them ideal destinations for boat tours and snorkeling adventures. Visitors have the opportunity to explore vibrant coral reefs, swim alongside schools of tropical fish, and even encounter sea turtles, dolphins, and rays in their natural habitat. Several operators in the region offer boat tours, ranging from half-day snorkeling trips to full-day excursions that include fishing, diving, and visits to secluded beaches. Snorkeling in the calm bays and around the rocky outcrops of the peninsula can be an unforgettable experience, revealing the underwater beauty of Costa Rica's Pacific coast. These tours not only offer the chance to witness the area's marine biodiversity but also provide unique perspectives of the coastline and its stunning landscapes.

To get the most out of your boat tour or snorkeling trip, book with reputable operators who prioritize safety and environmental conservation. The dry season, from December to April, generally offers the best conditions for snorkeling, with clearer waters and calmer seas. Be sure to bring sunscreen, a hat, and water, and consider wearing a rash guard for sun protection while snorkeling. Most tours provide all the necessary equipment, but if you have your own snorkel gear, you may prefer to use it for comfort and fit. Always follow your guide's instructions and respect the marine environment by not touching or standing on the coral.

Road Trip Around Nicoya Peninsula

Embarking on a road trip around the Nicoya Peninsula is an adventure that promises dramatic landscapes, hidden beaches, and authentic Costa Rican communities. The journey takes travelers through a diverse array of scenery, from rugged coastlines and tropical forests to small towns and agricultural lands. Driving in Nicoya offers the freedom to explore at your own pace, whether it's stopping for a spontaneous surf session, discovering a secluded waterfall, or enjoying fresh seafood at a beachside eatery.

The peninsula's road conditions can vary, with everything from well-paved highways to unpaved routes that require a 4x4 vehicle, especially during the rainy season. Planning your route in advance and staying updated on road conditions is crucial for a smooth journey. Renting a reliable vehicle and carrying a physical map or a GPS device with offline maps can help navigate remote areas where cell service may be spotty.

When planning a road trip around Nicoya, consider the season. The dry season offers easier driving conditions, while the green season presents lush landscapes but potentially challenging roads due to rain. Always carry plenty of water, snacks, and a first-aid kit, and make sure your vehicle has a spare tire and basic tools. Stopping at local markets and eateries not only enriches your travel experience but also supports the local economy.

Finally, be respectful of the environment and local communities by adhering to eco-friendly practices and exploring responsibly.

Guanacaste Cuisine

Guanacaste's cuisine is a vibrant expression of Costa Rica's culinary diversity, heavily influenced by its agricultural heritage and the bountiful Pacific Ocean. The region's traditional dishes reflect a harmonious blend of indigenous, Spanish, and African influences, creating flavors that are both unique and comforting. Staples include corn, used in a variety of forms from tortillas to tamales, and an abundance of fresh seafood, with ceviche being a popular choice along the coast. Rice and beans, the backbone of Costa Rican meals, take a local twist in Guanacaste with the addition of coconut milk in some recipes, adding a rich, tropical flavor.

One must-try dish is "arroz con pollo" (rice with chicken), a flavorful and hearty meal that is a favorite among locals and visitors alike. For those looking to explore Guanacaste's culinary landscape further, the region offers everything from upscale dining experiences showcasing modern interpretations of traditional dishes to simple sodas serving home-cooked meals.

When dining in Guanacaste, seek out local markets and festivals where you can sample a variety of dishes and ingredients unique to the region. Many restaurants and sodas also feature locally sourced produce, supporting sustainable agricultural practices. Don't miss the opportunity to try Guanacaste's renowned coffee, often served at the end of a meal. Ask your hosts or local residents for their dining recommendations, as they can lead you to hidden gems that offer authentic and delicious experiences.

Final Thoughts

Exploring Guanacaste and the Nicoya Peninsula offers a journey through some of Costa Rica's most stunning landscapes, vibrant communities, and rich cultural traditions. As you prepare to conclude your adventure in this remarkable region, consider taking a moment to reflect on the experiences that have shaped your visit. Whether it's the thrill of catching a perfect wave, the tranquility of a sunset on a secluded beach, or the warmth of the local people, Guanacaste provides memories that linger long after you've returned home.

For those who wish to delve deeper into the essence of Guanacaste, participating in community-led tours or volunteering with local conservation projects can offer meaningful insights into the region's environmental and cultural heritage. Guanacaste's diverse ecosystem, from its dry forests to marine reserves, underscores the importance of conservation efforts and sustainable tourism practices in preserving the natural beauty and biodiversity of the area.

As you venture beyond the well-trodden path, you may discover the soul of Guanacaste in its quiet villages, traditional festivals, and artisan workshops, each telling a story of resilience, creativity, and community. Embracing the Pura Vida spirit not only enriches your travel experience but also connects you to the heart of Costa Rica. Remember to travel responsibly, respecting the natural environments and local cultures that make Guanacaste a treasure to behold. Your journey through Guanacaste is more than a vacation; it's an opportunity to engage with a way of life that cherishes the land, the sea, and the community.

COSTA RICA TRAVEL GUIDE

CHAPTER 5:
Manuel Antonio National Park

Manuel Antonio National Park, nestled along Costa Rica's Pacific coast, is a jewel of natural beauty, renowned for its stunning beaches, lush rainforests, and an impressive array of wildlife. Despite being one of the smallest national parks in Costa Rica, Manuel Antonio packs a diverse ecosystem into its compact area, making it a popular destination for eco-tourists and nature lovers. The park's easy accessibility, combined with its scenic landscapes and biodiversity, offers a perfect blend of adventure and relaxation.

Visitors to Manuel Antonio can enjoy a range of activities, from hiking and wildlife watching to snorkeling and kayaking. The park also serves as an excellent example of Costa Rica's dedication to conservation and eco-tourism, with sustainable practices in place to protect its natural treasures. Whether you're exploring the park's trails, lounging on its pristine beaches, or discovering its marine life, Manuel Antonio provides an unforgettable experience that highlights the beauty of Costa Rica's natural world.

As you plan your visit, remember to respect the park's guidelines to minimize your environmental impact. The balance between enjoying the park's beauty and preserving its ecosystem is key to ensuring that Manuel Antonio remains a vibrant and thriving natural sanctuary for future generations.

Beaches of Manuel Antonio

Manuel Antonio National Park is home to some of Costa Rica's most picturesque beaches, renowned for their crystal-clear waters, powdery white sand, and scenic backdrops of lush greenery. Playa Manuel Antonio, the park's main beach, is a crescent-shaped bay perfect for swimming, sunbathing, and simply enjoying the breathtaking views. Nearby, Playa Espadilla Sur offers a more secluded atmosphere, ideal for those seeking tranquility amidst the park's natural beauty.

These beaches are not only idyllic retreats but also gateways to exploring the park's marine biodiversity, with snorkeling opportunities revealing colorful coral reefs and vibrant marine life. The juxtaposition of tropical forest and ocean ensures a refreshing and invigorating experience, with the sounds of the waves and wildlife creating a natural symphony.

To fully enjoy the beaches of Manuel Antonio, arrive early to secure a spot before the crowds. The park limits the number of visitors daily to protect the environment, so entering in the morning ensures access. Bring eco-friendly sunscreen, plenty of water, and snacks, but remember to take all your trash with you to keep the beaches pristine. Note that the park is closed on Tuesdays, planning your beach day accordingly.

Wildlife Watching

Manuel Antonio National Park is a haven for wildlife enthusiasts, offering one of the best opportunities in Costa Rica to observe a wide variety of animals in their natural habitat. The park's dense rainforest is home to iconic species such as sloths, howler monkeys, white-faced capuchins, and hundreds of bird species, including toucans and motmots. The park's biodiversity extends to its marine life, with dolphins and whales occasionally spotted off the coast.

Guided wildlife tours are highly recommended, as knowledgeable guides can spot and identify animals that might otherwise be missed. These tours not only enhance your understanding of the ecosystem but also emphasize the importance of conservation. Early morning or late afternoon are the best times for wildlife watching when animals are most active, and the heat is less intense.

When embarking on wildlife watching in Manuel Antonio, bring binoculars and a camera with a good zoom lens to capture close-up shots of the animals without disturbing them. Always maintain a respectful distance from wildlife and follow the park's rules to ensure a safe and enjoyable experience for everyone. Booking a guided tour in advance is advisable, especially during the peak tourist season, to secure your spot and gain deeper insights into the park's diverse ecosystems.

Catamaran Tours

Catamaran tours off the coast of Manuel Antonio offer an unparalleled opportunity to experience the beauty of the Pacific Ocean while enjoying the comfort and excitement of sailing. These tours provide a perfect blend of relaxation and adventure, allowing guests to sunbathe on the deck, snorkel in the clear waters, and often spot dolphins, sea turtles, and during certain seasons, even whales. The backdrop of Manuel Antonio's lush coastline adds to the serene experience, making it a must-do activity for visitors.

Many catamaran tours include amenities such as food and drinks, making for a comfortable day on the water. The snorkeling sessions offer a chance to dive into the underwater world of Costa Rica, exploring coral reefs and swimming alongside colorful fish. As the catamaran glides through the water, the crew shares insights about the local marine life and the area's ecological efforts to preserve its pristine condition.

When booking a catamaran tour, consider the size of the boat for a more personalized experience. Morning tours are great for those interested in snorkeling and wildlife watching, while sunset tours offer breathtaking views of the Pacific Ocean at dusk. Be sure to bring sunscreen, a hat, and a camera to capture the stunning scenery. Most operators provide all necessary snorkeling equipment, but it's always a good idea to confirm this in advance. Booking with eco-conscious tour operators that prioritize the environment and respect for marine life ensures that your adventure contributes positively to the area's sustainability efforts.

Mangrove Kayaking

Kayaking through the mangroves near Manuel Antonio is an adventurous way to connect with nature and explore one of the most unique ecosystems in Costa Rica. Paddling quietly along the waterways, visitors have the chance to observe a diverse array of wildlife, including birds, reptiles, and monkeys, in their natural habitat. The mangrove forests are vital to the ecological health of the area, acting as nurseries for marine life and protecting the coastline from erosion.

Guided tours are available and recommended for both novice and experienced kayakers. These tours not only ensure safety but also provide valuable information about the mangroves' biodiversity and the importance of their conservation. The tranquil waters and shaded canopies make for a serene paddling experience, suitable for all ages.

To make the most of your mangrove kayaking adventure, wear comfortable clothing that can get wet, and consider bringing water shoes. Early morning or late afternoon tours offer cooler temperatures and increased chances of wildlife sightings. Be sure to bring a waterproof bag for personal items and a camera, as the mangrove channels offer stunning photo opportunities. Booking with operators that practice sustainable tourism helps support the preservation of these critical environments for future generations.

Manuel Antonio by Night

Experiencing Manuel Antonio by night opens up a whole new world of nocturnal wildlife and vibrant nightlife. Nighttime jungle tours are an exciting way to see a different side of the park's ecosystem, with flashlights in hand and guided by experts, visitors can spot sleeping birds, nocturnal mammals like sloths and kinkajous, and various insects and amphibians that only emerge after dark. The sounds of the jungle at night create a mesmerizing ambiance, adding to the thrill of the adventure.

For those looking to enjoy the local nightlife, Manuel Antonio offers a variety of options, from beachfront bars and restaurants to lively clubs. The area's relaxed, tropical vibe makes it a great place to unwind after a day of exploring, with live music, dancing, and delicious cocktails.

When planning a night tour, wear long pants and closed-toe shoes to protect against insects and the terrain. It's advisable to book tours in advance, especially during the high season. For a night out in town, check with locals or your accommodation for recommendations on the best spots to experience Manuel Antonio's nightlife. Whether exploring the jungle's nocturnal life or enjoying the social scene, Manuel Antonio by night presents a captivating array of experiences.

Day Trip to Nauyaca Waterfalls

A day trip to Nauyaca Waterfalls from Manuel Antonio is an excursion into the heart of Costa Rica's stunning natural beauty. Located inland from the Pacific coast, Nauyaca Waterfalls are among the most breathtaking in the country, featuring two cascades that plunge into a serene pool perfect for swimming. The journey to the falls is an adventure in itself, traversing through lush landscapes and offering glimpses of local wildlife along the way.

Visitors can reach the waterfalls by a guided horseback riding tour, which adds an element of rustic charm to the experience, or by hiking along well-marked trails. The horseback tours often include a stop for a traditional Costa Rican breakfast, enhancing the cultural experience of the trip. The lower falls provide a natural swimming hole, inviting visitors to cool off with a refreshing dip in the clear, fresh waters beneath the cascading falls.

To visit Nauyaca Waterfalls, planning ahead is essential. The site charges an entrance fee, and booking a tour in advance is recommended, especially during peak tourist seasons. Wear comfortable, sturdy shoes and bring a swimsuit, towel, and waterproof camera or phone case to capture the majestic beauty of the falls. Remember to pack plenty of water and snacks for the journey, and consider visiting early in the morning to avoid crowds and fully enjoy the tranquility of this natural wonder.

Manuel Antonio Cuisine

Manuel Antonio's cuisine reflects the rich biodiversity of Costa Rica, offering a delightful array of fresh seafood, tropical fruits, and traditional dishes. The area's restaurants and eateries take full advantage of the coastal location, serving up everything from succulent ceviche to whole grilled fish, often accompanied by locally grown produce like plantains, yucca, and hearts of palm. International cuisine is also well-represented, with options ranging from Italian to Asian, ensuring there's something to satisfy every palate.

For an authentic taste of Manuel Antonio, try a "casado" – a typical Costa Rican meal consisting of rice, beans, salad, a choice of protein, and a side of fried plantains. Another must-try dish is "patacones" (fried green plantains), served with a variety of toppings or dips. The region's abundance of fresh coconuts means that coconut water and dishes featuring coconut milk are readily available and refreshing on a hot day.

When dining in Manuel Antonio, consider visiting restaurants that emphasize sustainable sourcing and support local fishermen and farmers. Many establishments proudly showcase their commitment to the environment and the community, offering not just a meal but an experience that connects you with the local culture and conservation efforts. Don't forget to pair your meal with a Costa Rican coffee or a tropical fruit smoothie for the perfect culinary conclusion to your day.

Hiking Trails in Manuel Antonio

Manuel Antonio National Park is not only known for its stunning beaches but also for its network of hiking trails that offer visitors the chance to explore the park's diverse ecosystems. From easy walks to more challenging hikes, the trails lead through dense rainforest, past tranquil lagoons, and up to panoramic viewpoints overlooking the Pacific Ocean. Each path reveals the park's rich biodiversity, including sloths, monkeys, iguanas, and a myriad of bird species.

The main trail, which winds its way from the entrance to the park's famed beaches, is well-maintained and suitable for hikers of all levels. For a more secluded experience, the Punta Catedral loop offers breathtaking views and a moderate challenge, while the waterfall trail provides a cooler, shaded hike with the reward of a beautiful waterfall at its end.

Before setting out on the trails, make sure to wear comfortable walking shoes and bring water, sunscreen, and insect repellent. Starting your hike early in the morning not only helps you beat the heat and the crowds but also increases your chances of wildlife sightings. Guided tours are available and recommended for those interested in learning more about the park's flora and fauna from expert local guides. Always stay on marked trails to protect the environment and ensure your safety in this beautiful but wild setting.

Conservation and Eco-Tourism Efforts

Manuel Antonio is a testament to Costa Rica's commitment to conservation and eco-tourism, showcasing how responsible travel practices can support the preservation of natural beauty and biodiversity. The area's efforts are centered around Manuel Antonio National Park, a jewel of conservation that protects rainforest, mangroves, coral reefs, and the myriad species that inhabit these ecosystems. Local businesses and tour operators adhere to eco-friendly practices, emphasizing sustainability in their operations, from minimizing waste to promoting the use of renewable resources.

Education plays a crucial role in these conservation efforts, with many tours and activities designed to enlighten visitors about the importance of environmental stewardship. Whether it's through guided nature walks that discuss the local ecosystem or wildlife viewing tours that adhere to ethical guidelines, the emphasis is always on respecting and protecting the natural world.

To contribute to these efforts, consider choosing accommodations and tours that have a proven commitment to sustainability. Look for certifications or affiliations with reputable conservation organizations. Additionally, practice responsible behavior during your visit by staying on marked trails, avoiding single-use plastics, and never feeding or disturbing wildlife. Your choices can have a positive impact, supporting the ongoing preservation of Manuel Antonio's irreplaceable natural heritage.

Final Thoughts

As your journey through Manuel Antonio comes to a close, you're left with a deeper appreciation for Costa Rica's natural wonders and a greater understanding of the importance of conservation. This beautiful corner of the world offers more than just picturesque beaches and lush rainforests; it presents an opportunity to engage with nature responsibly and sustainably.

Beyond the well-trodden paths, Manuel Antonio and its surrounding areas hold hidden treasures waiting to be explored, from secluded coves accessible only by kayak to quiet trails that offer intimate encounters with wildlife.

For those seeking to expand their exploration, consider visiting other nearby attractions such as the Damas Island Estuary for a mangrove boat tour or the lesser-known but equally stunning Playa Biesanz for a quiet beach day. Each experience in and around Manuel Antonio contributes to a tapestry of memories that highlight the beauty of Costa Rica and the importance of preserving it for future generations.

In leaving Manuel Antonio, carry forward the principles of Pura Vida and environmental stewardship in your travels and daily life. Share your experiences and the lessons learned about conservation with others, inspiring them to explore this incredible planet with respect and wonder. Manuel Antonio is not just a destination; it's a reminder of our collective responsibility to protect and cherish the natural world.

CHAPTER 6:
Corcovado National Park and the Osa Peninsula

· ·

The Osa Peninsula, with Corcovado National Park at its heart, is one of the most biodiverse places on Earth, offering an untouched paradise for nature lovers and adventure seekers alike.

This remote corner of Costa Rica is home to dense jungles, pristine beaches, and a wealth of wildlife, including many species that are rare or endangered. The commitment to conservation in this region ensures that its natural beauty and ecological diversity are preserved, providing a unique opportunity for eco-tourism and immersive nature experiences.

Visiting the Osa Peninsula and Corcovado National Park is a journey into the wild, where the lush rainforests meet the sparkling Pacific. The area's isolation contributes to its untouched beauty but also means that visits require careful planning and respect for the environment. It's a place where you can disconnect from the modern world and reconnect with nature, experiencing the raw power of the natural world.

As you prepare to explore this unparalleled destination, remember that the key to a fulfilling experience is to tread lightly and embrace the adventure. Whether hiking through Corcovado, snorkeling around Caño Island, or simply relaxing on a secluded beach, the Osa Peninsula offers a profound reminder of the wonders that await when we prioritize the preservation of our planet's natural treasures.

Hiking in Corcovado

Hiking in Corcovado National Park is an extraordinary experience, offering the chance to explore one of the last true wildernesses on the planet. The park's trails weave through various ecosystems, from lowland rainforests to mangrove swamps and cloud forests, each hosting a unique array of flora and fauna. This is the place to encounter Costa Rica's wildlife in its natural habitat, including tapirs, scarlet macaws, and the elusive jaguar. The park has several entry points and trails, ranging from day hikes to multi-day treks that require a guide. The La Leona, Sirena, and San Pedrillo stations serve as gateways to the park's wonders, with the Sirena Station offering the most remote and immersive jungle experience. Guided tours are not only recommended for safety but also enrich the hiking experience with expert knowledge of the park's biodiversity.

Planning your hike in Corcovado requires permits and reservations, especially if you intend to stay overnight at the Sirena Ranger Station. It's essential to book these well in advance due to the limited number of visitors allowed each day. Wear sturdy hiking shoes, bring plenty of water, and prepare for the park's humid conditions. Hiring a local guide not only supports the community but ensures you get the most out of your trek through this unparalleled ecosystem.

Dolphin and Whale Watching

The waters off the Osa Peninsula are a haven for marine life, providing exceptional opportunities for dolphin and whale watching. The area is one of the best in Costa Rica to witness the annual migration of humpback whales, which occurs from July to November for the northern hemisphere population and from December to March for whales from the southern hemisphere. Dolphins, including bottlenose, spinner, and spotted dolphins, are commonly seen year-round, making any trip to the Osa Peninsula a potential marine wildlife adventure.

Boat tours for dolphin and whale watching depart from various locations along the coast, guided by knowledgeable captains and guides who are adept at locating these magnificent creatures while respecting their natural behaviors. These excursions not only offer the thrill of seeing marine mammals up close but also provide insights into their ecology and the conservation efforts aimed at protecting them.

When booking a dolphin or whale-watching tour, look for responsible operators who adhere to guidelines that minimize disturbance to the animals. Early morning tours often provide the best conditions for sightings and smoother seas. Be sure to bring binoculars, a camera with a zoom lens, and sunscreen for your adventure. Contributing to conservation organizations that protect marine life in the Osa Peninsula can further enhance the positive impact of your visit.

Scuba Diving at Caño Island

Caño Island, located off the coast of the Osa Peninsula, is a premier destination for scuba diving enthusiasts seeking to explore Costa Rica's vibrant underwater world. The island's surrounding waters are designated as a biological reserve, protecting a spectacular array of marine life, including colorful coral reefs, schools of tropical fish, manta rays, sea turtles, and even sharks. The visibility is often excellent, ranging from 20 to 30 meters, making it an ideal spot for both novice and experienced divers.

Dive sites around Caño Island cater to a variety of skill levels, with some featuring gentle currents and shallow reefs, while others offer the chance to dive along deeper walls and pinnacles. The conservation status of the waters around the island means that interactions with marine life are frequent and memorable, offering a truly immersive experience in one of the world's most biodiverse marine environments.

To dive at Caño Island, it's necessary to book a tour with one of the licensed dive operators based in Drake Bay or Uvita. These tours typically include two dives, equipment rental, guides, and sometimes lunch. Ensure that the dive operator practices responsible tourism by respecting wildlife and the environment. It's advisable to bring a certification card and logbook if you have them. Diving during the dry season, from December to April, usually provides the best conditions. Remember, a portion of the tour fees goes towards conservation efforts, supporting the preservation of this marine sanctuary.

Wildlife Sanctuaries and Rescues

The Osa Peninsula is home to several wildlife sanctuaries and rescue centers dedicated to the rehabilitation and conservation of the region's diverse fauna. These centers play a critical role in caring for injured, orphaned, and confiscated animals with the goal of returning them to the wild whenever possible. Visiting these sanctuaries offers a unique opportunity to learn about Costa Rica's wildlife, the challenges they face, and the efforts made to protect them.

Sanctuaries such as the Osa Wildlife Sanctuary and Alturas Wildlife Sanctuary are open to visitors for guided tours that provide insights into the animals' behaviors, diets, and natural habitats. These tours not only educate visitors about conservation but also highlight the importance of ethical interactions with wildlife. The sanctuaries are home to a wide range of species, including monkeys, sloths, anteaters, and exotic birds, all of which are cared for in environments that mimic their natural habitats as closely as possible.

When planning a visit to a wildlife sanctuary, consider making a donation or purchasing items from their gift shops to support their conservation efforts. It's important to book your visit in advance and to follow all guidelines provided by the sanctuary to ensure the well-being of the animals. Photography is usually allowed, but flash should be avoided. These visits not only contribute to the financial support of the sanctuaries but also raise awareness about the significance of wildlife conservation in Costa Rica.

Corcovado by Night

Exploring Corcovado National Park by night is an adventure that reveals the nocturnal wonders of one of the most biodiverse places on earth. As darkness falls over the rainforest, a different set of inhabitants comes to life. Night tours in Corcovado offer the thrilling experience of navigating the jungle after dark, guided by the sounds of nocturnal creatures and the expertise of local guides who can spot and identify the myriad of species that are active at night.

These tours provide the rare opportunity to observe animals such as the elusive tapir, various species of bats, nocturnal birds like the owl, and a fascinating array of insects and amphibians that are not usually seen during daylight hours. The experience of walking through the rainforest at night, under the canopy of stars and the symphony of night sounds, is truly unforgettable and offers a deeper understanding of the complexity and beauty of the ecosystem.

Night tours in Corcovado require advance booking and are subject to park regulations and weather conditions. Wearing long pants, closed-toed shoes, and bringing insect repellent is recommended for comfort and protection. Participants should also bring a flashlight or headlamp, though it's important to follow the guide's instructions on when and how to use it to minimize disturbance to wildlife. Engaging in this unique experience not only heightens your appreciation for the natural world but also supports the ongoing conservation efforts within the park.

Boat Tours Around the Peninsula

Boat tours around the Osa Peninsula offer a splendid way to experience the pristine beauty of Costa Rica's Pacific coast from a different perspective. These excursions vary widely, ranging from leisurely coastal cruises to more adventurous snorkeling and diving trips that explore the rich marine ecosystems. One of the highlights is the opportunity to navigate the mangrove swamps, which are teeming with wildlife, including numerous bird species, reptiles, and occasionally, playful monkeys in the canopy above.

Many boat tours also skirt the edges of Corcovado National Park, providing a unique vantage point of the dense rainforest and its wildlife from the water. Dolphins are frequently seen frolicking in the boat's wake, and during certain seasons, whales can be spotted as they migrate through the warmer waters. Sunset cruises are particularly popular, offering breathtaking views of the sun dipping below the horizon, painting the sky in vibrant hues.

When selecting a boat tour, look for operators who emphasize ecological sensitivity and have knowledgeable guides. These professionals can enrich your experience by sharing insights into the local ecosystems and identifying wildlife. Ensure to bring sunscreen, a hat, and binoculars for birdwatching. Checking reviews and asking for recommendations can lead you to the best experiences. Remember, respecting the marine environment and keeping a safe distance from wildlife are paramount to preserving the beauty of the Osa Peninsula for future generations.

Osa Peninsula Road Trip

A road trip around the Osa Peninsula is an adventurous journey through some of Costa Rica's most untouched and rugged landscapes. The journey offers an array of experiences, from remote beaches and hidden waterfalls to small villages with welcoming locals. The roads can be challenging, with unpaved stretches and river crossings, adding to the adventure and requiring a reliable 4x4 vehicle. This journey isn't just about the destinations but the myriad of surprises and discoveries along the way.

Mapping out your route in advance is wise, though part of the adventure lies in the unexpected detours and stops. Places like

Drake Bay on the northern side of the peninsula or the quiet fishing village of Cabo Matapalo at the southern tip offer breathtaking natural beauty and serenity. These spots are perfect for those looking to escape the more touristy areas and immerse themselves in the natural world.

Preparation is key for a successful road trip on the Osa Peninsula. Ensure your vehicle is well-equipped for off-road conditions, carry plenty of water and snacks, and download offline maps or GPS for navigation. Check local travel advisories for weather conditions, especially during the rainy season when some roads may be impassable. Stopping at local eateries and engaging with communities along the way not only enriches your experience but also supports local economies. Remember, the essence of a road trip on the Osa Peninsula is in embracing the unexpected and reveling in the natural beauty that surrounds you.

Bird Watching in the Osa Peninsula

The Osa Peninsula is a paradise for bird watchers, home to more than 400 bird species, including several endemic and endangered species. The diverse habitats, from lowland rainforests to coastal mangroves, provide ample opportunities to observe a wide variety of birds, including the striking scarlet macaw, the elusive harpy eagle, and various species of toucans and hummingbirds. Early morning or late afternoon, when birds are most active, are the best times for bird watching.

Guided bird-watching tours can significantly enhance your experience, as local experts have an intimate knowledge of the area and can identify species by sight and sound. These guides can take you to the best spots for sightings and share insights into the behaviors and habitats of different bird species. For those passionate about avian photography, the Osa Peninsula offers unmatched opportunities to capture stunning images of these creatures in their natural environment.

To prepare for bird watching in the Osa Peninsula, bring binoculars with good magnification and a field guide to Costa Rican birds to help identify different species. Wearing camouflage or neutral-colored clothing can help blend into the surroundings and not startle the birds. Booking your stay or tours with eco-lodges and operators that support conservation efforts contributes to the preservation of the habitats that make the Osa Peninsula a bird-watching haven.

Osa Cuisine

The Osa Peninsula's cuisine is a delightful reflection of its rich biodiversity and the deep connection its people have with the land and sea. Local dishes are prepared with fresh, organic ingredients sourced directly from the surrounding forests and coastal waters. The culinary offerings in Osa are a fusion of traditional Costa Rican flavors with a unique twist, highlighting the peninsula's diverse cultural influences. Seafood, unsurprisingly, takes center stage, with fish, shrimp, and shellfish featuring prominently on menus, often accompanied by tropical fruits and vegetables grown in the area's fertile soil.

Restaurants and small eateries, known as sodas, serve up hearty casados, ceviches bursting with flavor, and rice dishes cooked with coconut milk, offering a taste of the local gastronomy. For those eager to dive deeper into the culinary culture, some lodges and tours offer cooking classes where you can learn to prepare traditional dishes using local techniques and ingredients.

When dining in the Osa Peninsula, seek out establishments that practice farm-to-table cooking, supporting local farmers and fishermen. This not only ensures the freshest meals but also contributes to the local economy and promotes sustainable agriculture and fishing practices. Don't miss the opportunity to try the local catch of the day or indulge in a refreshing tropical fruit smoothie. Ask your hosts or local residents for their dining recommendations to discover hidden culinary gems that offer an authentic taste of Osa.

Final Thoughts

As your adventure in the Osa Peninsula and Corcovado National Park comes to a close, it's clear that this corner of Costa Rica offers more than just a travel destination; it presents a profound connection to the natural world and a vibrant tapestry of life that calls for preservation and respect. The experiences you've collected here—whether trekking through lush rainforests, diving into the depths of the Pacific, or simply relishing the quiet moments on a secluded beach—serve as a reminder of the beauty and fragility of our planet.

For those inspired to further explore the wonders of the Osa Peninsula, consider extending your journey to include visits to local communities and artisan workshops where you can learn about traditional crafts and sustainable living practices. Engaging with the community not only enriches your travel experience but also fosters a deeper understanding of the cultural heritage and conservation efforts that define this unique region.

As you venture onward, carry with you the principles of responsible travel and the memories of the Osa Peninsula's untamed beauty. Share your stories, advocate for conservation, and support sustainable tourism initiatives that ensure the preservation of these natural treasures for future generations. The Osa Peninsula is a testament to the enduring allure of the wild, a place where adventure and conservation go hand in hand, offering endless opportunities for discovery and inspiration.

CHAPTER 7:
Caribbean Coast (Limon)

The Caribbean coast of Costa Rica, stretching from the northern wetlands of Tortuguero down to the laid-back beaches near the border with Panama, is a world apart from the rest of the country. This region boasts a rich cultural tapestry, blending Afro-Caribbean, Bribri Indigenous, and Costa Rican influences into a vibrant community with a unique way of life. Its lush rainforests, diverse wildlife, and picturesque beaches make it an unparalleled destination for nature lovers and those seeking to immerse themselves in a culturally rich environment.

The Caribbean coast is renowned for its relaxed pace, allowing visitors to truly disconnect and soak in the natural beauty and cultural heritage of the area. From the unparalleled biodiversity of its national parks to the rhythmic beats of calypso music that fill the air in its towns, Limon is a celebration of life, nature, and heritage.

As you explore the Caribbean coast, embrace the opportunity to step off the beaten path and experience the warmth of its people, the taste of its cuisine, and the untouched beauty of its landscapes. Whether you're navigating the canals of Tortuguero, surfing the waves of Puerto Viejo, or simply enjoying the tranquility of a remote beach, Limon offers an adventure that speaks to the soul.

Tortuguero National Park

Tortuguero National Park, often referred to as the "Amazon of Costa Rica," is a maze of waterways, lagoons, and dense rainforests that serve as a sanctuary for an astonishing variety of wildlife. Accessible only by boat or plane, the park's remote nature has helped preserve its pristine environment, making it one of the best places in Costa Rica for wildlife watching. Tortuguero is especially famous for its sea turtle nesting beaches, where, depending on the season, visitors can witness the incredible sight of turtles laying their eggs or hatchlings making their first journey to the sea.

The park offers guided boat tours through its network of canals, providing close encounters with monkeys, sloths, crocodiles, and numerous bird species. These tours are conducted by local guides with a deep knowledge of the ecosystem, ensuring a rich and educational experience. The village of Tortuguero, located just outside the park, provides a cultural complement to the natural wonders, with opportunities to learn about the local way of life and conservation efforts.

Visiting Tortuguero National Park requires planning, as accommodations and tours should be booked in advance, especially during the turtle nesting season from July to October. Waterproof clothing, insect repellent, and binoculars are essential items for your visit. Supporting local eco-lodges and hiring local guides not only enhances your experience but also contributes to the community's economy and conservation efforts.

Cahuita National Park and Black Beach

Cahuita National Park is a gem on the Caribbean coast, known for its stunning coral reefs, diverse marine life, and lush coastal rainforests. The park is home to White Beach (Playa Blanca), renowned for its powdery white sand, and Black Beach (Playa Negra), famous for its striking black volcanic sand. Visitors can explore the park's trails, which offer easy hikes through the forest leading to secluded beaches where the jungle meets the sea.

Snorkeling in the waters off Cahuita National Park is a must-do activity, offering a chance to observe the vibrant coral and fish species that inhabit the area. The park's coral reef is one of the most accessible in Costa Rica, with guided snorkeling tours available to ensure a safe and environmentally respectful experience.

Admission to Cahuita National Park is by a voluntary donation, which contributes to its maintenance and conservation. The park is open year-round, but the best time for snorkeling is during the dry season, from February to April, when visibility is highest. Remember to bring sun protection, water, and snacks for your hike, and consider hiring a local guide at the park entrance to learn more about the wildlife and ecosystems you'll encounter. Supporting the park's conservation efforts and respecting wildlife guidelines are essential for preserving this natural paradise.

Surfing in Puerto Viejo

Puerto Viejo, with its laid-back Caribbean vibe and stunning coastal scenery, is a surfers' paradise known for its powerful waves and vibrant surf culture. The town's most famous break,

Salsa Brava, is renowned for its heavy barrels, attracting experienced surfers from around the world. However, Puerto Viejo and its surroundings also offer a variety of breaks suitable for all skill levels, from gentle waves ideal for beginners to challenging swells for the pros.

The surf scene in Puerto Viejo is as much about the water as it is about the community. Local surf shops offer board rentals and lessons, and the camaraderie among surfers is palpable. After a day in the surf, the town's eclectic mix of restaurants and bars provides the perfect backdrop for sharing stories and relaxing with fellow wave chasers.

For those looking to hit the waves, the best time to surf in Puerto Viejo is from November to April, when the swells are most consistent. It's advisable to check the surf forecast and speak with local surfers or instructors to find the best spots for your skill level. Remember to respect the local surf etiquette and the environment by avoiding coral reefs and using reef-safe sunscreen. Supporting local businesses by renting equipment or taking lessons from local surf schools not only enhances your experience but also contributes to the community.

Snorkeling and Diving in Cahuita

Cahuita offers some of the most accessible and beautiful snorkeling and diving experiences on Costa Rica's Caribbean coast, thanks to the stunning coral reefs of Cahuita National Park. The park's protected waters are home to an impressive diversity of marine life, including colorful fish, sea turtles, and various species of coral. The clear, calm waters make for excellent visibility, providing an underwater spectacle that's easily enjoyed by snorkelers and divers alike.

Guided snorkeling and diving tours are available and recommended, not only for safety reasons but also to ensure the protection of the coral reefs. Experienced guides can lead you to the best spots and share their knowledge about the marine ecosystem, enhancing your underwater adventure. These tours often include equipment rental, making it easy for travelers to explore the underwater wonders without needing to bring their gear.

The best time for snorkeling and diving in Cahuita is during the dry season, from February to April, when the sea is calmest and visibility is at its peak. Remember to book your tour with eco-friendly operators who practice responsible tourism to minimize impact on the reef. Conservation is a priority in Cahuita, and by choosing responsible tour operators, visitors can contribute to the ongoing efforts to protect this invaluable marine ecosystem.

Rainforest Excursions in Veragua

The Veragua Rainforest Reserve offers an immersive experience into the heart of Costa Rica's lush rainforests, just a short drive from the Caribbean coast. This research and adventure park provides a unique blend of education and adventure, with aerial tram rides, zip-lining, and guided walking tours through the forest. The reserve is dedicated to the conservation of the region's biodiversity and offers visitors the chance to see a wide variety of flora and fauna, including exotic birds, colorful frogs, and perhaps even the elusive sloth.

Veragua's highlight is the aerial tram, which takes visitors on a serene journey above the rainforest canopy, offering spectacular views and the opportunity to spot wildlife from a unique perspective. The reserve also features a butterfly garden, a frog habitat, and a research station where visitors can learn about the ongoing scientific work to study and protect the rainforest's inhabitants.

Planning a visit to Veragua Rainforest Reserve involves choosing the activities that interest you most, as the reserve offers several packages. It's advisable to wear comfortable walking shoes and bring insect repellent, sunscreen, and a rain jacket, as weather conditions in the rainforest can change quickly. Supporting Veragua's conservation efforts by visiting the reserve not only provides an unforgettable experience but also contributes to the important research and educational programs that help protect Costa Rica's rainforests.

Gandoca-Manzanillo Wildlife Refuge

The Gandoca-Manzanillo Wildlife Refuge represents a significant portion of Costa Rica's commitment to preserving its natural treasures. Situated along the southern Caribbean coast, this refuge encompasses a variety of ecosystems, from lowland rainforests and mangroves to coral reefs and seagrass beds. It's a haven for wildlife enthusiasts, offering the chance to observe a wide array of species in their natural habitat, including howler monkeys, sloths, and a myriad of bird species, as well as the endangered manatee.

One of the highlights of visiting the Gandoca-Manzanillo Wildlife Refuge is the opportunity to explore its pristine beaches and hike through the jungle trails that offer breathtaking views of the Caribbean Sea. The refuge's coral reefs are also accessible for snorkeling, providing a glimpse into the vibrant underwater life that thrives in these protected waters.

To visit, it's best to engage with local guides who can lead you through the refuge's trails and share insights into the conservation efforts and the ecology of the area. The best times for wildlife spotting are early morning or late afternoon when animals are most active. Remember to respect the environment by staying on designated paths, not disturbing the wildlife, and taking all trash with you. Visiting the refuge not only offers a profound connection with nature but also supports the local community and conservation initiatives.

Caribbean Coast by Night

The Caribbean coast of Costa Rica transforms as the sun sets, offering a vibrant nightlife scene that reflects the unique culture of this region. From the lively bars and clubs in Puerto Viejo to the more laid-back beach bonfires and gatherings in smaller towns, there's something for everyone to enjoy. The mix of reggae, calypso, and dancehall music fills the air, inviting locals and visitors alike to dance and enjoy the night.

Night markets and cultural events frequently take place, showcasing the art, music, and cuisine of the Caribbean coast. These events provide a wonderful opportunity to experience the local culture and interact with community members. Additionally, night tours, such as guided walks to observe nocturnal wildlife or sea turtle nesting excursions, offer unique experiences that highlight the natural beauty of the area under the cover of darkness.

When planning to enjoy the Caribbean coast by night, consider the type of experience you're looking for and check local listings for events or tours. Always prioritize safety by staying in well-lit areas and going out in groups. Engaging with the nightlife is not only a chance to relax and have fun but also an opportunity to support local businesses and appreciate the diverse cultural influences that make the Caribbean coast unique.

Day Trip to Bribri Indigenous Reserves

A day trip to the Bribri Indigenous Reserves offers a profound and educational experience, providing insight into the lives, traditions, and knowledge of one of Costa Rica's indigenous communities. Located in the lush rainforests of the Talamanca region, these reserves are home to the Bribri people, who maintain a close relationship with the land, practicing sustainable agriculture and preserving their cultural heritage.

Visitors have the opportunity to learn about Bribri customs, language, and connection to nature through guided tours that often include visits to cacao plantations, traditional homes, and medicinal gardens. The Bribri are known for their cacao production, and participating in a cacao processing demonstration is a highlight, revealing the importance of this crop both culturally and economically.

Engaging with the Bribri community through respectful and responsible tourism supports their efforts to preserve their way of life and share their knowledge with others. It's important to book these tours through reputable operators that work directly with the community, ensuring that your visit benefits the Bribri people. Bring an open mind and be prepared to embrace a different pace of life, respecting the customs and guidelines shared by your hosts. This immersive experience not only enriches your understanding of Costa Rica's cultural diversity but also contributes to the sustainable development of indigenous communities.

Caribbean Coast Cuisine

The cuisine of Costa Rica's Caribbean coast is a flavorful testament to the region's cultural diversity, blending Afro-Caribbean, Indigenous, and Spanish influences into a unique culinary experience. Dishes here are often centered around coconut, spices, and fresh seafood, offering a distinct taste that sets it apart from other Costa Rican fare. One iconic dish is "Rondón," a hearty stew made with coconut milk, fish, and whatever else is available, embodying the improvisational spirit of Caribbean cooking.

Another staple is the "rice and beans" cooked with coconut milk, unlike its counterpart in other parts of Costa Rica, served alongside spicy chicken or fish, and flavored with Panamanian pepper and other local spices. For those with a sweet tooth, the Caribbean coast offers an array of desserts made from tropical fruits, coconut, and spices, providing a sweet conclusion to any meal.

To truly savor the Caribbean coast cuisine, seek out local sodas and eateries that serve traditional dishes. Markets and street food vendors are also excellent places to sample local flavors and snacks. Engaging with the food is engaging with the culture, and visitors are encouraged to ask about the history and preparation of their meals, offering a deeper appreciation for the culinary traditions of the region.

Final Thoughts

Your journey along the Caribbean coast of Costa Rica is more than just a travel experience; it's an immersion into a vibrant tapestry of natural beauty, rich culture, and culinary delights. As you reflect on your time spent exploring lush rainforests, relaxing on pristine beaches, and engaging with the local communities, remember that this unique region offers lessons in conservation, diversity, and sustainability.

For those looking to extend their adventure, consider exploring the lesser-known areas of the Caribbean coast, such as the hidden waterfalls and secluded beaches accessible only by foot or boat, offering a sense of discovery and solitude. Participating in community-led tours and workshops can also provide insights into local art, agriculture, and environmental conservation, enriching your understanding of the region's ethos.

As you depart from the Caribbean coast, carry with you the spirit of Pura Vida and a commitment to preserving the natural and cultural heritage you've been privileged to experience. Share your stories, advocate for the protection of these precious environments, and consider how you can incorporate the principles of sustainability and respect for diversity into your daily life. The Caribbean coast is a reminder of the beauty that flourishes when we live in harmony with nature and each other, inspiring us to create a more conscious and connected world.

COSTA RICA TRAVEL GUIDE

CHAPTER 8:
Costa Rican Cuisine

Costa Rican cuisine is a vibrant reflection of the country's rich cultural heritage, agricultural bounty, and diverse ecosystems. Known for its emphasis on fresh, locally sourced ingredients, Costa Rican food is both nutritious and delicious, offering a variety of flavors that appeal to a wide range of palates. At the heart of Costa Rican meals are rice and beans, complemented by a variety of fruits, vegetables, meats, and seafood, which are prepared using methods that have been passed down through generations.

This cuisine is characterized by its simplicity and reliance on the natural flavors of the ingredients. Whether you're enjoying a meal in a bustling city eatery or a rural family kitchen, the food is prepared with care and served with pride. Costa Rica's commitment to sustainable and organic farming practices means that meals are not only tasty but also environmentally conscious.

Exploring Costa Rican cuisine is an integral part of experiencing the country's culture. From the ubiquitous gallo pinto to the hearty casado, each dish tells a story of Costa Rica's history, traditions, and the everyday life of its people. As you delve into the flavors of Costa Rica, you'll discover that the nation's culinary landscape is as diverse and beautiful as its rainforests and beaches.

Gallo Pinto

Gallo pinto, meaning "spotted rooster" in Spanish, is Costa Rica's national dish and a staple of the local diet. This flavorful mix of rice and black beans is seasoned with onions, bell peppers, cilantro, and a splash of Salsa Lizano, a uniquely Costa Rican sauce that adds a tangy, slightly sweet flavor. Traditionally served as a breakfast dish alongside eggs, tortillas, sour cream, and fried plantains, gallo pinto provides a hearty start to the day, fueling Costa Ricans for their daily activities.

The beauty of gallo pinto lies in its versatility and the personal touch each cook brings to the recipe. While the basic ingredients remain constant, regional variations and family recipes add diversity to this beloved dish. In the Caribbean region, for example, coconut milk is sometimes added to the rice, giving it a distinctive flavor and richness.

To truly appreciate gallo pinto, try it in a local soda, where it's often prepared with love and served as part of a traditional Costa Rican breakfast. Making gallo pinto at home is also a simple and satisfying way to bring a taste of Costa Rica into your kitchen. Experimenting with the amount of Salsa Lizano or adding a personal twist to the recipe can make your gallo pinto uniquely yours. Remember, the key to a great gallo pinto is the quality of its ingredients, so use the freshest produce and beans you can find.

Casado

The casado is the quintessential Costa Rican lunch, offering a balanced and nutritious meal that reflects the country's agricultural abundance. Translating to "married man" in Spanish, the casado traditionally includes a protein—such as chicken, fish, beef, or pork—accompanied by rice, beans, salad, a slice of fried plantain, and often a side of tortillas or cheese. The combination of ingredients in a casado represents a marriage of flavors that is both satisfying and wholesome.

Each component of the casado plays a crucial role in creating a harmonious dish. The protein is typically grilled or stewed, seasoned with Costa Rican spices and herbs. The beans and rice provide a hearty base, while the salad—made with fresh vegetables—adds a refreshing contrast. The sweet plantain brings a touch of sweetness that complements the savory elements perfectly.

To experience the diversity of casado, visit different sodas and restaurants across Costa Rica, as each place offers its unique take on this traditional dish. For travelers looking to immerse themselves in local cuisine, a casado provides a delicious insight into the everyday eating habits of Costa Ricans. When ordering a casado, don't hesitate to ask for the day's special or the chef's recommendation to enjoy the freshest and most flavorful options.

Ceviche

Ceviche, a beloved dish throughout Latin America, holds a special place in Costa Rican cuisine, celebrated for its fresh, zesty flavors. This delightful seafood dish is made by marinating raw fish or seafood in citrus juices, typically lime or lemon, which effectively "cooks" the protein. The Costa Rican version often includes finely chopped cilantro, onion, bell pepper, and sometimes tomato, all contributing to its vibrant taste and texture. The key to an exceptional ceviche is the freshness of the ingredients, with coastal regions of Costa Rica offering some of the best due to their access to daily catches.

While ceviche is commonly enjoyed as an appetizer or a light meal, it's more than just food; it's a social dish, often shared among friends and family at gatherings or enjoyed as a refreshing treat after a day at the beach. The simplicity of ceviche belies the depth of its flavor, making it a must-try for any visitor to Costa Rica.

For those eager to try their hand at making ceviche, local fish markets are the best place to source fresh fish or seafood. Experimenting with the balance of citrus, salt, and herbs can lead to a personalized version that suits your palate. For an authentic Costa Rican experience, enjoy your ceviche with a cold Imperial beer or a glass of chilled white wine, ideally in a beachside setting where the ocean breeze complements the dish's fresh flavors.

Tropical Fruits and Smoothies

Costa Rica's tropical climate and fertile lands yield an abundance of exotic fruits, making it a paradise for fruit lovers. Markets and roadside stalls overflow with vibrant offerings like mangoes, pineapples, papayas, guanábanas (soursop), and the unique pejibayes (peach palms), among others. These fruits not only provide a delicious snack or dessert but are also the basis for another Costa Rican staple: the smoothie. Blended with ice, water, or milk, these fruit smoothies, known locally as "batidos," offer a refreshing escape from the tropical heat.

Exploring the local markets provides an opportunity to discover and taste fruits you may not find elsewhere. Vendors are usually happy to explain how to eat the more exotic varieties or suggest the best fruits for making smoothies. The richness of Costa Rican soil imparts exceptional sweetness and flavor to its fruits, enhancing both the eating and drinking experience.

When in Costa Rica, don't pass up the chance to start your day with a tropical fruit smoothie or incorporate some of the local fruits into your meals. For a truly immersive experience, participate in a cooking class or a farm tour where you can learn more about the cultivation of these fruits and their role in Costa Rican cuisine and culture. Remember, consuming local fruits not only supports local farmers but also reduces the carbon footprint associated with food transport.

Coffee and Chocolate

Costa Rica's coffee and chocolate are products of the country's rich volcanic soil and favorable climate, embodying a tradition of quality and sustainability. Costa Rican coffee is renowned worldwide for its exceptional quality, characterized by a smooth, medium body, and a balanced flavor profile with hints of fruit and cocoa. The coffee culture here is deep-rooted, with the daily ritual of the "cafecito" uniting friends, families, and communities. Visiting a coffee plantation offers insights into the meticulous process of coffee production, from planting and harvesting to roasting, and is an essential experience for any coffee enthusiast.

Similarly, Costa Rica's chocolate industry has flourished, with a focus on organic, artisanal production that honors the country's biodiversity. Cacao, once considered the "food of the gods" by Indigenous peoples, is now transformed into high-quality chocolate bars, truffles, and other confections that are as rich in flavor as they are in history. Chocolate tours provide a hands-on experience, from bean to bar, allowing visitors to participate in the chocolate-making process and understand the importance of sustainable practices in cacao cultivation.

To fully appreciate the depth and variety of Costa Rican coffee and chocolate, seek out local cafés and chocolatiers that source their beans directly from local farmers. Tasting sessions and workshops are not only enjoyable but also offer the chance to learn about the nuances that define these exquisite products. Supporting small-scale producers and cooperatives directly contributes to the livelihood of local communities and the preservation of Costa Rica's environmental heritage.

Local Dining Spots

Discovering local dining spots is a journey into the heart of Costa Rican culture, where the essence of Pura Vida is served on a plate. From the bustling sodas found in every town and city to the hidden gems tucked away in rural areas, these local eateries offer authentic and delicious Costa Rican meals at affordable prices. Sodas, in particular, are family-run establishments that pride themselves on serving traditional dishes like casado, arroz con pollo, and gallo pinto, made with recipes passed down through generations.

Exploring these local dining spots not only allows you to taste the country's culinary diversity but also provides an opportunity to interact with local residents and learn about their way of life. Many of these establishments use locally sourced ingredients, supporting the community's farmers and producers, and contributing to the sustainability of the local food system.

To fully experience the richness of Costa Rican cuisine, ask for the day's special or a recommendation when visiting a soda or local restaurant. This could lead you to discover dishes that are not commonly found on tourist menus but are cherished by locals. Remember, dining in these places is not just about the food; it's about embracing the Costa Rican way of life, where meals are a time for sharing and enjoyment. Carry cash, as some smaller spots may not accept credit cards, and be open to trying new flavors and dishes that embody the country's culinary heritage.

Food Festivals

Food festivals in Costa Rica are vibrant celebrations of the country's rich culinary heritage, offering a feast for the senses. These events are not only about savoring delicious dishes but also about experiencing Costa Rica's diverse cultures and traditions. From the Chocolate Festival in Puerto Viejo, celebrating the region's deep connection to cacao, to the Seafood Festival in Puntarenas, highlighting the bounty of Costa Rica's waters, each festival is a unique opportunity to delve into the flavors that define different regions of the country.

Attending these festivals allows visitors to sample a wide range of dishes, from traditional Costa Rican fare to innovative culinary creations by local chefs. It's also a chance to watch cooking demonstrations, participate in tastings, and even learn how to prepare local dishes. Beyond the food, these festivals often include music, dance, and other cultural performances, making them a comprehensive cultural experience.

When planning to attend a food festival in Costa Rica, check the event's schedule in advance and arrive early to beat the crowds. These festivals are popular among locals and tourists alike, and some of the best dishes can sell out quickly. Bringing a reusable water bottle and bag can help minimize waste, supporting the festivals' efforts to be environmentally friendly. Food festivals in Costa Rica are not just about eating; they're about celebrating the country's agricultural wealth, culinary creativity, and communal spirit.

Regional Specialties

Costa Rica's diverse geography, ranging from the Caribbean coast to the Central Valley and the Pacific shores, has given rise to a variety of regional specialties that reflect the unique characteristics of each area. On the Caribbean side, dishes are infused with coconut milk and spices, offering a distinct flavor profile exemplified by rice and beans cooked in coconut oil. The Central Valley, with its rich volcanic soil, produces an abundance of vegetables and dairy products, influencing dishes like olla de carne, a hearty beef and vegetable stew.

Exploring regional specialties is an adventure in itself, providing insights into how geography, climate, and cultural influences shape local cuisines. In Guanacaste, the influence of cattle ranching is evident in the popularity of beef dishes, while the Southern Pacific coast is renowned for its seafood, including ceviche made with the freshest catch.

To truly savor the diversity of Costa Rican cuisine, seek out local markets and festivals, where regional specialties are proudly on display. Don't hesitate to ask locals for recommendations on where to find the best examples of their regional dishes. This not only leads to delicious culinary discoveries but also fosters connections with the local community, enriching your travel experience. Whether it's sampling fresh cheese in Monteverde, enjoying a plate of Caribbean chicken in Limón, or tasting the catch of the day on the Pacific coast, each regional specialty tells a story of Costa Rica's rich cultural tapestry and abundant natural resources.

Vegetarian and Vegan Cuisine

Costa Rica's abundant natural resources and commitment to sustainability have made it a haven for vegetarian and vegan cuisine. The country's rich volcanic soil yields a diverse array of fruits and vegetables, which form the basis of many Costa Rican dishes. Vegetarian and vegan visitors will find a variety of options, from traditional dishes adapted to meet dietary preferences to innovative meals created with plant-based ingredients. Tropical fruits, legumes, grains, and an array of fresh vegetables are staples in Costa Rican kitchens, offering flavorful and nutritious options for every meal.

Restaurants specializing in vegetarian and vegan cuisine are becoming increasingly common, particularly in tourist areas and larger cities. Many traditional eateries, or sodas, are also accommodating to vegetarians and vegans, often willing to modify dishes upon request. The national dish, gallo pinto, is naturally vegan, and casados can easily be adapted by substituting meat or fish with grilled vegetables or a vegetable stew.

To enjoy Costa Rica's vegetarian and vegan cuisine, look for establishments that highlight local and organic produce. Farmers' markets are excellent places to sample fresh fruits and vegetables and to discover the incredible variety of produce that Costa Rica has to offer. Don't hesitate to ask about the ingredients in dishes and express any dietary preferences; Costa Ricans are known for their hospitality and willingness to accommodate guests. Enjoying the vegetarian and vegan cuisine in Costa

Rica is not only a delight for the palate but also a way to support sustainable and ethical eating practices.

Final Thoughts

As your culinary journey through Costa Rica comes to an end, you're left with a taste of the country's rich biodiversity, cultural diversity, and commitment to sustainability. Costa Rican cuisine offers a window into the nation's soul, from its humblest sodas serving traditional fare to innovative restaurants pushing the boundaries of local cuisine. The freshness of the ingredients, the simplicity of the preparation, and the warmth of the Costa Rican people combine to create meals that are nourishing in every sense.

For those seeking to delve deeper into Costa Rica's culinary landscape, consider participating in a cooking class or visiting a coffee plantation or organic farm to see firsthand where the country's delicious ingredients come from. Beyond the plate, Costa Rica's culinary traditions tell a story of ecological richness, cultural intersections, and a forward-looking approach to sustainability.

As you reflect on your experiences, remember that every meal shared, every new flavor discovered, and every story told around the table contributes to a deeper understanding and appreciation of Costa Rica. Carry these flavors and memories with you, and let them inspire not only a love for Costa Rican cuisine but also a respect for the principles of sustainability and community that it embodies. Whether you're savoring a cup of rich Costa Rican coffee at home or preparing a dish inspired by your travels, the essence of Pura Vida remains with you, a reminder of the beauty, diversity, and richness of life in Costa Rica.

CHAPTER 9:
How to Travel on a Budget in Costa Rica

Traveling to Costa Rica on a budget is entirely possible, with careful planning and smart choices allowing you to enjoy the richness of this beautiful country without breaking the bank. Costa Rica's appeal lies in its stunning natural landscapes, abundant wildlife, and friendly locals, all of which can be experienced without spending a fortune. The key to budget travel here is flexibility, research, and a willingness to embrace the pura vida lifestyle in a way that might mean bypassing luxury resorts in favor of more authentic, cost-effective options.

Budget travelers can take advantage of Costa Rica's extensive public transportation network, affordable local eateries, and a variety of free or low-cost activities that highlight the country's natural beauty and cultural heritage. From hiking in national parks to swimming at some of the world's most beautiful beaches, many of Costa Rica's treasures don't cost a thing to enjoy.

To make the most of your trip while staying on budget, start by outlining your priorities, whether they're wildlife watching, adventure sports, or simply soaking in the natural hot springs scattered throughout the country. With a bit of creativity and flexibility, you can tailor a Costa Rican adventure that's both memorable and affordable, proving that the richness of the experience doesn't have to be determined by the price.

Choosing the Right Time to Visit

One of the most effective strategies for traveling on a budget in Costa Rica is choosing the right time to visit. The country's peak tourist season, running from December to April, coincides with the dry season, offering sunny days and minimal rainfall. However, this is also when prices for accommodations, tours, and even some goods and services can be at their highest due to increased demand. To save money, consider visiting during the "green season," from May to November, when rainfall is more common but prices significantly drop, and crowds thin out.

The green season brings its own set of advantages, including lush landscapes, more active wildlife, and the opportunity to experience Costa Rica's rainforests at their most vibrant. Additionally, many tour operators and accommodations offer discounts during this time, making it easier to stretch your budget further. While afternoon rains are common, mornings are often sunny and clear, providing ample time for exploration.

When planning your visit, also keep an eye on holiday periods and local festivals, which can affect availability and prices. Traveling just outside of peak times or major holidays can result in considerable savings while still allowing you to enjoy good weather and all the activities Costa Rica has to offer.

Accommodation

Accommodation is one of the most significant expenses when traveling, but in Costa Rica, there are plenty of budget-friendly options that don't compromise on the experience. Hostels are widely available and offer not only affordable beds but also the chance to meet fellow travelers. Many hostels provide private rooms in addition to dorms, catering to those who prefer a bit more privacy. For a more immersive experience, consider homestays or small guesthouses, where you can enjoy local hospitality and often, home-cooked meals.

Another cost-effective option is camping or staying in eco-lodges, particularly in or near national parks. These accommodations can offer a closer connection to nature and a truly unique experience at a fraction of the cost of luxury resorts. Websites and apps that specialize in vacation rentals can also be excellent resources for finding deals on apartments and houses, especially if traveling in a group.

To maximize savings on accommodation, book well in advance, especially if traveling during the high season or around holidays. Don't hesitate to contact accommodations directly to ask about discounts for longer stays or off-season rates. Remember, part of the adventure is where you stay, and choosing budget-friendly accommodations can lead to discoveries and experiences that enrich your travel story in Costa Rica.

Food and Drinks

Eating on a budget in Costa Rica doesn't mean you have to compromise on taste or experience. The country's culinary scene offers plenty of affordable options that allow you to savor local flavors without a hefty price tag. Traditional sodas, small, family-owned restaurants, are ubiquitous and serve hearty Costa Rican meals at a fraction of the cost of tourist-oriented establishments. Here, you can enjoy dishes like gallo pinto, casado, and arroz con pollo, which are not only delicious but also give you a genuine taste of local cuisine.

Street food is another budget-friendly option, offering everything from fresh tropical fruit to empanadas and ceviche. Markets and food festivals present opportunities to sample a variety of dishes and snacks at low prices. Additionally, cooking for yourself can save money, especially if staying in accommodations with kitchen facilities. Local markets and supermarkets offer fresh, local ingredients that you can use to prepare your meals, allowing for a fun and economical way to experience Costa Rican food culture.

To save on food and drinks, carry a reusable water bottle to take advantage of the country's potable tap water, and consider packing snacks for day trips to avoid paying premium prices at tourist spots. Exploring local eateries outside of main tourist areas can also lead to lower prices and more authentic dining experiences. Embracing the local eating habits, such as the substantial midday meal followed by a lighter dinner, can further help stretch your food budget while traveling in Costa Rica.

Transportation

Transportation costs in Costa Rica can vary widely, but with some planning, it's possible to navigate the country on a budget. Public buses are the most economical way to travel between cities and towns, offering a reliable and affordable means to explore. Though journeys can be long, the buses reach nearly every destination in the country, providing a scenic, if slower, alternative to more expensive private transfers or domestic flights.

For those looking to explore more remote areas or enjoy the flexibility of their itinerary, renting a car might be a viable option. Sharing rental costs with fellow travelers can make this a cost-effective choice. However, be sure to consider the type of vehicle you'll need, as some areas require a 4x4, and always check for the best rental deals and insurance requirements before booking.

Biking is another budget-friendly transportation option in smaller towns and rural areas, particularly on the Caribbean coast and around some national parks. Bike rentals are relatively inexpensive and offer a leisurely way to explore the natural beauty of Costa Rica. Whichever mode of transportation you choose, always weigh the cost against the convenience and safety, and don't hesitate to mix and match options to suit your budget and travel style.

Sightseeing and Attractions

Costa Rica is a playground for nature lovers and adventurers, many of whom are delighted to discover that the country's best sights often come with little to no cost. National parks and reserves charge an entrance fee, but these are generally reasonable and contribute to conservation efforts. Planning your visit to include several parks or natural attractions can maximize the value you get from each entrance fee. Additionally, some lesser-known parks offer similar experiences to their more famous counterparts but at a lower cost.

Free attractions abound if you know where to look. Beaches, for instance, are free and open to the public, offering endless hours of relaxation or surfing. Many communities also have public gardens, plazas, and walking paths that provide insight into local life and culture without costing a dime. For a deeper dive into Costa Rica's rich biodiversity, consider joining a free or donation-based walking tour in areas known for their natural beauty.

Maximizing your sightseeing budget also means taking advantage of any discounts available for students, seniors, or children, and keeping an eye out for combo tickets that offer reduced rates for multiple attractions. Planning your sightseeing around central locations can minimize transportation costs, while always being on the lookout for community events or festivals, which can offer free or inexpensive entertainment and cultural experiences. Embracing the natural and cultural wealth of Costa Rica doesn't have to be expensive; with a little creativity and flexibility, you can experience the country's top attractions on a budget.

Shopping

Shopping in Costa Rica can be a delightful experience that doesn't necessarily have to strain your budget. Local markets and artisan shops are treasure troves of unique finds, from handcrafted jewelry and pottery to vibrant textiles and delicious local coffee. These places offer the chance to purchase authentic souvenirs while supporting local artisans and producers. When shopping, it's wise to compare prices at different stalls or shops, as you can often find the same or similar items at varying prices. Bargaining is acceptable in some markets, but it's important to do so respectfully and with a sense of fairness, keeping in mind that many vendors rely on these sales for their livelihood. For groceries and everyday items, local supermarkets and farmer's markets can provide lower prices than convenience stores in tourist areas, allowing you to try local flavors and ingredients without overspending.

To make the most of your shopping experience, set a budget for souvenirs and gifts, and stick to it. Carrying a list of items you're interested in can help keep your shopping focused and prevent impulse buys. Remember, the best souvenirs are often those that hold personal significance or support local craftsmanship, rather than the most expensive items on the shelf.

Avoiding Tourist Traps

Tourist traps, while common in popular destinations worldwide, can be avoided in Costa Rica with some foresight and local knowledge. Typically, these traps involve overpriced services, attractions, or items that don't offer genuine value or cultural experience. Researching and planning your activities in advance can safeguard against falling into these traps, as can seeking out recommendations from locals or fellow travelers who have firsthand insights into the area's best offerings.

One effective strategy is to dine where the locals eat, visit attractions that are not solely geared towards tourists, and shop in local markets rather than souvenir shops clustered around major tourist sites. This approach not only helps you avoid tourist traps but also enriches your travel experience by immersing you in the local culture and supporting the community.

Always be cautious of unsolicited offers or tours from individuals on the street, and book activities through reputable companies, even if it means paying a bit more. The assurance of quality and safety often outweighs the potential cost savings of a deal that seems too good to be true. Being mindful of these details can enhance your enjoyment of Costa Rica, letting you experience the country's authentic charm without unnecessary expenses.

Using Local Currency

In Costa Rica, the local currency is the colón, and while US dollars are widely accepted in tourist areas, using local currency can often lead to better prices and smoother transactions. Familiarizing yourself with the exchange rate before your trip can help you make informed decisions when paying for goods and services. It's also advisable to have colones on hand for small purchases, such as at local markets, street vendors, or rural areas where dollars might not be readily accepted.

Withdrawing local currency from ATMs upon arrival is a convenient option, though it's wise to check with your bank regarding international transaction fees. Exchanging a small amount of money at the airport can cover immediate expenses, but better exchange rates are usually found at banks or authorized exchange offices in larger towns and cities.

Carrying small denominations can facilitate easier transactions and tipping, reducing the need for vendors to make change. Being mindful of where and how you exchange money, and choosing to use colones for day-to-day expenses, can contribute to a more authentic and cost-effective experience in Costa Rica. Managing your money wisely, being aware of exchange rates, and opting for local currency when possible can all play a part in traveling smartly and sustainably.

Travel Insurance

Investing in travel insurance for your trip to Costa Rica is a wise decision that can provide peace of mind and financial protection. While Costa Rica is generally a safe destination, unexpected events such as illness, injury, or travel disruptions can happen. Comprehensive travel insurance covers medical expenses, which is crucial since medical care, although excellent, can be costly for tourists. It can also cover losses due to theft or damage to personal belongings, as well as trip cancellations or interruptions.

When selecting travel insurance, look for policies that cover activities you plan to engage in, such as adventure sports, which might require additional coverage. Read the fine print to understand the extent of the coverage, including any deductibles and exclusions. It's also helpful to choose a policy that offers 24-hour assistance for emergencies.

Purchasing travel insurance well in advance of your trip ensures that you are covered for any pre-trip incidents that might cause you to cancel, such as illness. Always carry a copy of your insurance policy and contact numbers for your insurance company while traveling. In the end, the small cost of insurance is a worthwhile investment against the backdrop of unforeseen expenses, ensuring that your budget travel plans remain intact.

Bargaining

Bargaining can be part of the shopping experience in Costa Rica, especially in markets and street vendor settings. However, it's important to approach bargaining with respect and understanding, recognizing that many sellers depend on their earnings for their livelihood. The key is to negotiate prices in a friendly and polite manner, without being overly aggressive or disrespectful. Not all items will have negotiable prices, particularly in formal stores or establishments with clearly marked prices.

A good practice is to start by asking the price and then, if you feel it's high, offer a lower amount that you think is fair. Keep in mind that the goal is to reach a price that is acceptable to both you and the seller, not to undercut the value of the item or service. Being fluent in some basic Spanish phrases can also be advantageous in bargaining situations, as it shows respect for the local culture and can sometimes lead to better outcomes.

Remember, while bargaining is accepted in some contexts, it's not appropriate everywhere. Observing others and asking local advice can give you a sense of where and when bargaining is acceptable. Ultimately, bargaining should be seen as part of the cultural exchange, offering a way to interact with locals and learn more about the value of goods and services in Costa Rica.

Final Thoughts

Traveling to Costa Rica on a budget is not only possible but can also enrich your travel experience, encouraging a deeper engagement with the country's culture, people, and natural beauty. By planning ahead, choosing the right time to visit, and being mindful of your spending on accommodation, food, transportation, and activities, you can enjoy a memorable trip without overspending. Embracing local experiences, from dining at sodas to exploring national parks, allows you to see the heart of Costa Rica while supporting the local economy and conservation efforts.

Being flexible, open to new experiences, and willing to step off the beaten path can lead to unexpected discoveries and opportunities to connect with locals. Remember, the essence of Costa Rica's pura vida lifestyle lies not in luxury or extravagance but in appreciating the simple joys and natural wonders that the country has to offer.

As you reflect on your journey and plan future travels, consider how the lessons learned in Costa Rica about sustainability, conservation, and community can inform your approach to travel elsewhere. Costa Rica's commitment to preserving its natural beauty and fostering a culture of inclusivity and respect offers valuable insights for travelers seeking to explore the world in a responsible and enriching manner.

CHAPTER 10:
10 Cultural Experiences You Must Try in Costa Rica

Experiencing the rich tapestry of Costa Rican culture is about more than just enjoying its natural wonders; it's about immersing oneself in the country's vibrant traditions, flavors, and daily life. Costa Rica, a land known for its pura vida philosophy, offers a plethora of cultural experiences that allow visitors to connect with its history, people, and the essence of what makes this country unique. From the joyous celebrations at local festivals to the serene moments spent in the heart of a coffee plantation, each experience provides a deeper understanding of Costa Rica's heritage and contemporary lifestyle.

Engaging in these cultural experiences not only enriches your travel adventure but also fosters a greater appreciation for the diversity and resilience of the Costa Rican spirit. Whether it's learning about indigenous cultures, participating in conservation efforts, or simply savoring the local cuisine, these experiences offer insights into the values and traditions that have shaped this vibrant nation.

As you embark on this journey through Costa Rica's cultural landscape, remember to approach each experience with an open heart and mind. Embracing the pura vida way of life means more than just enjoying the beauty of the land; it's about connecting with its people, understanding their history, and participating in their customs and daily activities.

1. Attending a Local Festival

Costa Rica's local festivals are a kaleidoscope of color, music, and tradition, offering a lively window into the country's cultural heritage. From the spirited Carnival in Limón to the historical reenactments at the Día de los Cultures in October, these festivals celebrate Costa Rica's diverse cultural roots, including indigenous, Spanish, and Afro-Caribbean influences. Attending a local festival allows you to experience firsthand the communal spirit and joy that characterize Costa Rican celebrations. Festivals often include parades, traditional dances, music performances, and, of course, an array of local cuisine. The Puntarenas Carnival, for example, transforms the coastal city into a vibrant party, while the Fiestas Palmares in January is one of the largest and most anticipated events, featuring rodeos, concerts, and fireworks. Each festival has its unique charm and offers a glimpse into the local community's values and traditions.

To fully enjoy these festivals, research the dates and locations in advance, as many are annual events with specific significance to their communities. Wear comfortable clothing and shoes, as you'll likely be on your feet for extended periods, and don't forget to bring a camera to capture the festivities. Participating in a local festival is not just about observing; it's an invitation to join in the celebration, sample traditional foods, and maybe even learn a few dance steps, making it a truly immersive cultural experience.

2. Exploring a Coffee Plantation

Coffee is not just a beverage in Costa Rica; it's a way of life and a symbol of the country's agricultural heritage. Exploring a coffee plantation offers insight into the meticulous process of coffee production, from planting and harvesting to roasting and brewing. Tours typically include a walk through the plantation, an explanation of the coffee-making process, and, of course, a tasting session where you can savor the rich flavors of freshly brewed Costa Rican coffee.

The Central Valley, with its ideal climate and elevation, hosts some of the country's most renowned coffee plantations. Visiting these plantations, you'll learn about the history of coffee in Costa Rica and its significance to the national economy and culture. Many plantations are still family-owned and operated, with generations of knowledge and passion poured into every cup.

When choosing a coffee plantation tour, look for those that emphasize sustainable farming practices and fair labor conditions, as these reflect the growing trend towards environmental stewardship and social responsibility in the coffee industry. Booking a tour in advance can ensure a spot, especially during the harvest season from November to January. Exploring a coffee plantation is not only a journey through the scenic landscapes of Costa Rica but also an opportunity to connect with the land and people that produce one of the world's finest coffees.

3. Visiting an Indigenous Reserve

Costa Rica is home to several indigenous reserves, where communities strive to preserve their ancestral heritage, languages, and traditions. Visiting an indigenous reserve offers a unique opportunity to learn about the country's original cultures and their deep connection to the natural world. These visits can include guided tours, cultural presentations, and even hands-on experiences with traditional crafts, agriculture, and culinary practices. The Bribri in the Talamanca region, for example, share their knowledge of medicinal plants, cacao cultivation, and the significance of their spiritual practices.

When planning a visit to an indigenous reserve, it's important to approach the experience with respect and sensitivity. Many communities welcome visitors as a way to share their culture and history, but it's crucial to engage in these exchanges through reputable organizations or guides who have established relationships with the communities. This ensures that your visit contributes positively to the community and provides an authentic and respectful cultural exchange.

Before your visit, research the specific customs and guidelines for visitors, as each community may have its own protocols. Dress modestly, ask permission before taking photographs, and consider purchasing crafts or products directly from the community as a way to support their local economy. Visiting an indigenous reserve is a profound experience that not only enriches your understanding of Costa Rica's cultural diversity but also highlights the importance of preserving these cultures for future generations.

4. Wildlife Watching in National Parks

Costa Rica's national parks are renowned for their incredible biodiversity, making wildlife watching one of the country's must-have experiences. From the elusive jaguars and vibrant scarlet macaws of Corcovado National Park to the mischievous capuchin monkeys and sloths of Manuel Antonio, each park offers a unique window into the rich tapestry of life that thrives in these protected areas. Guided tours by experienced naturalists enhance the experience, providing insights into the habits and habitats of the diverse species you'll encounter.

The key to a rewarding wildlife watching experience is patience and respect for the natural environment. Early mornings or late afternoons are often the best times to observe animals when they are most active. Staying quiet and maintaining a safe distance ensures minimal disturbance to the wildlife and increases your chances of spotting the more timid species.

Choosing eco-friendly tours and adhering to park rules, such as staying on marked trails and not feeding the animals, are essential practices that support conservation efforts and ensure the sustainability of wildlife tourism. Bringing binoculars and a good camera with a zoom lens can capture the magic of these encounters for years to come. Wildlife watching in Costa Rica's national parks is not just an activity; it's an immersion into a world where nature's complexity and beauty are on full display.

5. Zip Lining Through the Forest

Zip lining in Costa Rica offers an exhilarating perspective of the country's lush landscapes and incredible biodiversity, all while soaring above the treetops. Born in Costa Rica, zip lining was initially developed for scientists to study inaccessible forest canopies, but it has since become a popular activity for adventure seekers. The experience allows participants to glide across canyons, rivers, and through the forest at speeds that elevate the heart rate and the spirit.

Safety is paramount, and reputable companies adhere to strict standards, providing thorough instructions and high-quality equipment. Tours often include multiple zip lines, offering various lengths and heights that cater to thrill-seekers and cautious adventurers alike. Some zip lines even offer unique experiences like superman cables, where you're harnessed face down to simulate flight, or night zip lining for a nocturnal adventure.

When selecting a zip lining tour, research and choose operators with excellent safety records and positive reviews. Wear comfortable clothing, closed-toed shoes, and secure any loose items. Embracing this adventure not only pumps adrenaline but also fosters a deeper appreciation for the majesty of Costa Rica's forests from a bird's-eye view. Zip lining through the forest encapsulates the essence of Costa Rican adventure tourism, blending excitement with the natural beauty that defines this country.

6. Relaxing in Hot Springs

Costa Rica's volcanic landscape offers not just dramatic scenery but also the soothing luxury of natural hot springs. Nestled amidst lush foliage and offering views of towering volcanoes, these thermal waters are believed to have healing properties, rich in minerals and perfect for relaxation. From the renowned springs near Arenal Volcano to more secluded spots hidden in the country's verdant interior, there's a range of experiences to suit every preference, from rustic to resort-style.

The hot springs provide a tranquil retreat where visitors can unwind after a day of hiking or adventure activities. Many of the hot springs facilities incorporate natural elements into their design, creating pools and waterfalls that blend seamlessly with the surrounding environment. For a truly immersive experience, some locations offer spa treatments, mud baths, and other wellness services that utilize the mineral-rich waters.

When planning a visit to the hot springs, consider your budget and the type of experience you're looking for, as entry fees and amenities can vary widely. Visiting during the week or outside peak hours can offer a more peaceful experience. Don't forget to bring a swimsuit, water, and a change of clothes. Relaxing in Costa Rica's hot springs is not only a chance to soak in the country's natural beauty but also to embrace the pura vida lifestyle, prioritizing relaxation and wellness.

7. Surfing on Both Coasts

Costa Rica is a surfer's paradise, with its Pacific and Caribbean coasts offering waves for every level of surfer, from beginners to seasoned pros. The Pacific coast is famed for its consistent breaks, with spots like Tamarindo, Santa Teresa, and Jacó attracting surfers from around the world. Meanwhile, the Caribbean coast, particularly around Puerto Viejo, boasts the legendary Salsa Brava, known for its powerful waves. Each coast has its unique charm and challenges, providing a diverse surfing experience.

Local surf schools and instructors are available at most popular surf spots, offering lessons and board rentals. For beginners, these schools provide a safe and supportive environment to learn the basics, while more experienced surfers can gain local knowledge about the best times and places to catch the perfect wave. Surfing in Costa Rica is not just about the sport; it's about connecting with the ocean and the laid-back surf culture that embodies the spirit of pura vida.

When planning your surfing adventure, consider the time of year, as seasons affect wave conditions. The Pacific coast generally offers the best surfing from May to November, while the Caribbean side is optimal from December to March. Always respect the local surf etiquette, take care of the natural environment by using reef-safe sunscreen, and, most importantly, embrace every moment spent in the water. Surfing on both of Costa Rica's coasts provides a thrilling way to explore the country's stunning beaches and coastal communities.

8. Participating in a Turtle Release Program

One of the most rewarding and impactful experiences in Costa Rica is participating in a sea turtle release program. Various beaches along both coasts serve as nesting sites for several species of endangered sea turtles, including the leatherback, hawksbill, and green turtle. Conservation organizations and local communities often run programs where volunteers can help protect nests, monitor hatching turtles, and assist in safely guiding the hatchlings to the ocean. This hands-on conservation work not only contributes to the survival of these magnificent creatures but also offers a profound connection to the natural world.

These programs often include educational components, teaching participants about the life cycle of sea turtles, the threats they face, and the importance of conservation efforts. Witnessing the journey of these tiny hatchlings as they make their first trek to the sea is an unforgettable experience, filled with hope and a deep sense of responsibility toward protecting our planet's biodiversity.

To participate in a turtle release program, research and connect with reputable conservation organizations that offer volunteer opportunities. These programs can vary in length, from a single evening to several weeks, and may require a fee or donation that supports the organization's conservation efforts. Booking in advance is crucial, especially during peak nesting or hatching seasons. Participating in a turtle release program is a chance to make a positive impact while experiencing one of Costa Rica's most inspiring natural phenomena.

9. Hiking to Waterfalls

Hiking to one of Costa Rica's many breathtaking waterfalls is an experience that combines physical activity with the tranquil beauty of nature. The country's diverse landscape, marked by lush rainforests and rugged mountains, is home to countless water-falls, ranging from towering cascades to serene, hidden pools. These hikes not only provide a chance to immerse oneself in Costa Rica's stunning natural environments but also to cool off with a refreshing swim in crystal-clear waters at the journey's end. Popular waterfall destinations include La Fortuna Waterfall near Arenal Volcano, with its impressive drop and large swim-ming hole, and the Nauyaca Waterfalls in the southern region, known for their dramatic beauty and the opportunity for cliff jumping. Each hike offers a unique glimpse into the country's ecosystem, showcasing the flora and fauna that thrive in these moist environments.

When planning a waterfall hike, it's essential to wear appropri-ate footwear, as trails can be slippery and uneven. Bringing a swimsuit, towel, and waterproof camera will ensure you're pre-pared to enjoy the water and capture the moment. Many waterfalls are accessible via guided tours, which can provide additional insights into the area's ecology and history. Embarking on a hike to a Costa Rican waterfall is not just a walk in the woods; it's an adventure that refreshes the body and spirit.

10. Sampling Traditional Costa Rican Cuisine

Delving into traditional Costa Rican cuisine is a must-have cultural experience for any visitor. The country's culinary traditions reflect its agricultural abundance and cultural diversity, offering flavors that are both simple and richly satisfying. From the staple gallo pinto at breakfast to a diverse casado for lunch, each dish tells a story of Costa Rica's history and its people's connection to the land. Sampling these dishes provides a taste of the local lifestyle, seasoned with the pura vida spirit.

For a truly immersive experience, consider participating in a cooking class where you can learn to prepare traditional dishes using local ingredients. Many of these classes are held in picturesque settings, from rural farms to urban markets, providing a backdrop that enhances the culinary journey. Additionally, visiting local markets offers the opportunity to taste fresh fruits and vegetables unique to the region, such as pejibaye (peach palm fruit) and guanábana (soursop), and to see firsthand the bounty that inspires Costa Rican cuisine.

To embrace the full spectrum of Costa Rican cuisine, be adventurous in your selections. Try the savory empanadas, savor the sweet tres leches cake, and don't miss out on the rich, locally produced coffee. Dining in Costa Rica is an opportunity to connect with the country's culture, landscape, and people, one delicious bite at a time.

Final Thoughts

Exploring the must-have cultural experiences in Costa Rica offers an adventure that goes beyond the surface of this vibrant country. From the adrenaline of zip lining through the forest canopy to the serene moments spent in natural hot springs, each experience contributes to a deeper understanding and appreciation of what makes Costa Rica truly unique. The journey through Costa Rica's cultural landscape is as diverse as its ecosystems, offering something for every traveler, whether you're drawn to its natural wonders, culinary delights, or the warmth of its people.

As you reflect on your adventures, remember that the essence of the Costa Rican experience lies in the pura vida philosophy—a celebration of life's simple joys and an appreciation for the natural beauty that surrounds us. Carry this spirit with you as you continue your travels or return home, letting the memories of your time in Costa Rica inspire a lifelong connection to nature, culture, and the pursuit of happiness. This journey through Costa Rica's cultural experiences is not just a chapter in your travel story; it's an invitation to embrace life with joy, curiosity, and an open heart.

CHAPTER 11:
Recommended Itinerary in Costa Rica

Embarking on an adventure in Costa Rica offers a vibrant exploration of its lush landscapes, rich biodiversity, and cultural depth. This journey is designed to immerse you in the essence of pura vida—the pure life philosophy that pulses through the heart of Costa Rica.

From the bustling streets of San José to the misty tranquility of Monteverde, the fiery spectacle of Arenal, and the pristine beaches of Manuel Antonio, this itinerary unfolds a tapestry of experiences that resonate with the spirit of adventure and discovery. Here, every turn reveals a new horizon, every day brings a connection to nature, and every encounter shares a story of conservation and community.

Planning Your Trip

To ensure a seamless Costa Rican adventure, thoughtful planning is crucial. Start by considering the time of year; the dry season (December to April) promises sunny skies and vibrant wildlife, making it ideal for exploring beaches and rainforests, though it's also the peak tourist season. The green season (May to November) unveils a lush, verdant landscape with fewer crowds, offering a more intimate experience with nature, albeit with the possibility of rain.

When booking flights, compare options for arriving at Juan Santamaría International Airport (San José) or Daniel Oduber Quirós International Airport (Liberia), depending on your itinerary start point. Domestic travel within Costa Rica blends efficiency with adventure—choose between short regional flights, comprehensive bus networks, or car rentals for flexibility. Packing for Costa Rica means preparing for diversity; include lightweight rain gear, sturdy footwear for hiking, swimwear, and sun protection. Finally, ensure your itinerary includes a blend of activities reflecting Costa Rica's natural wonders, cultural richness, and conservation efforts, setting the stage for an unforgettable journey.

7-Day Itinerary in Costa Rica

Day 1: Arrival in San José - City Tour

Your Costa Rican odyssey begins in San José, a city where the past and present converge amidst vibrant markets, historic neighborhoods, and an array of museums. Upon arrival, settle into your accommodation and prepare to explore the heart of the nation. A guided city tour can offer insights into Costa Rica's rich cultural heritage and modern-day vibrancy. Key stops should include the ornate National Theatre, a beacon of Costa Rican culture and artistry; the Pre-Columbian Gold Museum, housing an impressive collection of indigenous gold artifacts; and the bustling Central Market, offering a taste of local life and cuisine.

San José's array of restaurants and cafés serve as gateways to Costa Rican flavors, making dinner an ideal time to sample traditional dishes like casado or gallo pinto. As night falls, consider a stroll through lively neighborhoods like Barrio Escalante, where craft beer bars and chic eateries offer a warm welcome. This first day is about acclimatization, embracing the city's rhythm, and anticipating the natural splendors that await.

Day 2: Arenal Volcano and Hot Springs

Rise early and set out for La Fortuna, the gateway to Arenal Volcano, a symmetrical cone that stands as a testament to Costa Rica's volcanic activity. The journey itself is a scenic introduction to the country's diverse ecosystems. Upon arrival, explore the Arenal Volcano National Park (referenced in Chapter 2), where trails offer close views of the volcano and lava fields from past eruptions. The surrounding rainforest is alive with the sounds of wildlife, presenting opportunities to spot toucans, howler monkeys, and coatis.

After a day of exploration, unwind in one of La Fortuna's natural hot springs. Fed by geothermal activity beneath the Arenal Volcano, these springs range from luxurious resorts with landscaped pools to more secluded, natural settings. This experience, is the perfect way to relax muscles sore from hiking and immerse yourself in the verdant beauty of Costa Rica's landscapes.

Day 3: Monteverde Cloud Forest Reserve

An early departure will take you to the Monteverde Cloud Forest Reserve (referenced in Chapter 3), a world-renowned biodiversity hotspot. The cooler temperatures and misty conditions of this elevated forest create a unique habitat for thousands of plant species, hundreds of bird species, and myriad insects and mammals, including the elusive Resplendent Quetzal. Start your visit with a guided walk to learn about the delicate ecosystem and conservation efforts that maintain this natural treasure.

In the afternoon, embrace adventure with a canopy tour, featuring zip lines and hanging bridges that offer exhilarating views of the forest from above. Monteverde's commitment to sustainable tourism and conservation is evident in these activities, which are designed to minimize environmental impact while maximizing visitor engagement with the natural environment.

Day 4: Travel to Manuel Antonio - Beach Time

Journey from the cloud-shrouded heights of Monteverde to the sun-kissed shores of Manuel Antonio (referenced in Chapter 5). This leg of your trip unveils the Pacific Coast's dramatic landscapes, where mountains meet the sea. Upon arrival, spend the afternoon lounging on one of Manuel Antonio's pristine beaches, such as Playa Espadilla or the more secluded Playa Biesanz. The warm, turquoise waters invite swimming and snorkeling, offering a refreshing counterpoint to the cloud forest's cool embrace.

As the sun begins to set, take a leisurely walk along the beach or enjoy a cocktail at a beachfront bar, reflecting on the journey thus far. Manuel Antonio's relaxed atmosphere and natural beauty set the stage for the adventures that await in the national park. This transition from highland forests to tropical coastline exemplifies Costa Rica's incredible geographical and ecological diversity, offering a glimpse into the country's rich array of landscapes and experiences.

Day 5: Explore Manuel Antonio National Park

Dedicate your fifth day to exploring Manuel Antonio National Park, a jewel of conservation renowned for its stunning beaches, lush rainforest, and diverse wildlife. Start your day early to beat the crowds and increase your chances of wildlife encounters. The park's trails are well-maintained and offer varying levels of difficulty, ensuring that everyone, from avid hikers to families, can enjoy the experience. Keep an eye out for sloths, iguanas, and the colorful but mischievous capuchin monkeys. Don't forget to pack water, snacks, and binoculars for birdwatching.

After a morning of exploration, relax on one of the park's beautiful beaches, such as Playa Manuel Antonio, a picturesque cove ideal for swimming and sunbathing. Reflect on the conservation efforts that have preserved this natural paradise, a recurring theme in your journey through Costa Rica's protected areas.

Day 6: Return to San José - Coffee Plantation Tour

On your return to San José, a visit to a coffee plantation offers a delightful insight into one of Costa Rica's most important exports and cultural staples. The Central Valley, with its ideal climate and elevation for coffee cultivation, is home to numerous plantations that welcome visitors. Engage in a tour to learn about the journey of coffee from bean to cup, as mentioned in Chapter 1.

These tours often include walking through the coffee fields, observing the milling and roasting process, and, of course, tasting the final product. This experience not only provides a deeper appreciation for your morning brew but also highlights the importance of sustainable agricultural practices.

Spend your final evening in San José enjoying the culinary delights and vibrant atmosphere of the city. Whether you're revisiting a favorite spot or trying something new, it's a chance to toast to the adventures and memories of the past week.

Day 7: Departure or Day Trip Options

Depending on your departure time, your last day might allow for one final adventure. For those with a late flight, consider a day trip to explore more of the Central Valley's riches.

Options include visiting the Poás Volcano National Park, with its impressive crater and cloud forest, or the vibrant artisan town of Sarchí, known for its hand-painted oxcarts. Both destinations offer a glimpse into Costa Rica's natural and cultural beauty, rounding out your experience. If your journey extends beyond a week, Costa Rica still has much more to offer. Here's how you could spend three additional days exploring its rich landscapes and culture.

10-Day Itinerary in Costa Rica

Day 8: Visit the Poás Volcano National Park

Should your travels allow for a longer stay, a visit to Poás Volcano National Park presents an excellent start to your extended itinerary. One of the country's most active volcanoes, Poás offers a rare opportunity to peer into an enormous crater with a turquoise sulfuric lake. The park also features trails that lead through cloud forests to another, extinct crater now filled with a serene lake. Remember, the park limits visitor numbers for safety and conservation reasons, so booking your entry ticket in advance is advisable.

After exploring Poás, consider stopping by La Paz Waterfall Gardens on your way back to San José. This privately owned eco-park features not only spectacular waterfalls but also a wildlife rescue center with an aviary, butterfly observatory, and a variety of Costa Rican animals.

Day 9: Cultural Day in San José

Dedicate another day to delving deeper into the cultural heart of Costa Rica by exploring San José further. Visit the Jade Museum to view the largest collection of pre-Columbian jade artifacts in Latin America, highlighting the rich indigenous heritage of the region. Art enthusiasts should not miss the Costa Rican Art Museum, housed in a striking building that was the country's first international airport terminal.

In the evening, explore the Escazú area, known for its colonial architecture and contemporary dining scene. Here, you can enjoy a fusion of traditional Costa Rican flavors with international cuisine, reflecting the cosmopolitan side of San José.

Day 10: Day Trip to Tortuguero National Park

For a final adventure, consider a day trip to Tortuguero National Park on the Caribbean coast. Known as the "Amazon of Costa Rica," Tortuguero is a network of waterways, lagoons, and dense rainforest, making it accessible only by boat or plane. It's famous for its sea turtle nesting beaches, with the chance to see turtles laying eggs or hatchlings making their way to the ocean, depending on the season.

A guided boat tour through the canals offers sightings of diverse wildlife, including monkeys, crocodiles, and a plethora of bird species. The remote, unspoiled beauty of Tortuguero provides a fitting conclusion to an extended exploration of Costa Rica, encapsulating the country's commitment to preserving its natural wonders.

Additional Itinerary Ideas for Exploring Costa Rica

For those drawn to the allure of Costa Rica and seeking to tailor their adventure beyond the suggested itinerary, the country's diverse landscapes and vibrant culture offer endless possibilities for exploration and discovery. Imagine beginning your journey on the Caribbean coast, where the laid-back rhythm of life and the rich Afro-Caribbean heritage infuse every experience, from the spicy flavors of the local cuisine to the sound of reggae that floats on the evening breeze. In places like Cahuita and Puerto Viejo, you can immerse yourself in the vibrant coral reefs, relax on pristine beaches, and delve into the heart of the Gandoca-Manzanillo Wildlife Refuge, a haven for wildlife and a testament to Costa Rica's commitment to conservation.

Venture inland, and the majestic peaks of the Talamanca Range beckon with the promise of adventure. Here, among the cloud-kissed mountains, lies the hidden valley of San Gerardo de Dota, a paradise for bird watchers and nature lovers, where the elusive Resplendent Quetzal can be spotted. The area's pristine rivers and waterfalls invite contemplation and connection with the natural world, offering a serene counterpoint to the coastal experience.

For those interested in cultural immersion, the Guanacaste region presents an opportunity to experience the traditions of Costa Rican ranch life. Participate in a "sabanero" (cowboy) experience, learning about the local way of life, cattle ranching, and the conservation of dry tropical forest. Guanacaste's beaches are among the best in the country for surfing, providing both novice and experienced surfers with world-class waves against a backdrop of stunning sunsets.

Adventurous souls may be drawn to the rugged beauty of the Nicoya Peninsula, with its remote beaches and vibrant surf culture. Here, you can explore the bohemian charm of towns like Montezuma and Santa Teresa, practice yoga overlooking the Pacific, or embark on a quad bike adventure to discover hidden beaches and waterfalls.

Lastly, for a truly off-the-beaten-path experience, consider a journey to the Osa Peninsula, where the wild heart of Costa Rica beats strongest. Described by National Geographic as "the most biologically intense place on Earth," this region offers unparalleled opportunities for wildlife watching, hiking in pristine rainforests, and experiencing the raw power and beauty of untouched nature.

Costa Rica's myriad landscapes and experiences invite travelers to craft their journey, whether seeking adventure, relaxation, cultural immersion, or a blend of all three. Each path taken reveals the depth and richness of this incredible country, promising memories that will last a lifetime and a deeper appreciation for the natural world and the cultures that thrive within it. For those who seek further adventure or wish to tailor their Costa Rican journey to specific interests, the possibilities are endless. Whether you're drawn to the allure of untouched beaches, the call of the wild, or the depth of cultural immersion, Costa Rica's diverse landscape caters to every traveler's dream. Below are several itinerary ideas to inspire your travel plans, offering a blend of exploration, relaxation, and adventure across this vibrant country.

1. The Surfer's Quest (**7 DAYS**)

- Day 1 & 2: Jacó – Surf lessons and beach exploration

- Day 3 & 4: Santa Teresa – Advanced surfing and yoga sessions

- Day 5: Dominical – Surfing and visiting Nauyaca Waterfalls

- Day 6 & 7: Pavones or Playa Hermosa – Surfing in some of the world's longest left-hand waves

2. Wildlife and Nature Expedition (**10 DAYS**)

- Day 1 & 2: Tortuguero National Park – Canal tours and turtle nesting (seasonal)

- Day 3 & 4: Sarapiquí – Rainforest hikes and whitewater rafting

- Day 5 & 6: Monteverde Cloud Forest Reserve – Bird-watching and canopy tours

- Day 7 & 8: Corcovado National Park – Wildlife watching and guided jungle treks

- Day 9 & 10: Marino Ballena National Park – Snorkeling and whale watching (seasonal)

3. Costa Rican Culture Deep Dive (**7 DAYS**)

▶ Day 1 & 2: San José – City tour, museums, and cultural performances

▶ Day 3: Sarchí – Visiting artisan workshops and oxcart factories

▶ Day 4 & 5: Guanacaste – Exploring traditional ranches (Haciendas) and learning about cowboy culture

▶ Day 6: Cartago – Visiting the Basilica of Our Lady of the Angels and exploring the Orosi Valley

▶ Day 7: San Gerardo de Dota – Coffee plantation tour and birdwatching

4. Ultimate Relaxation Retreat (**7 DAYS**)

▶ Day 1 & 2: La Fortuna – Hot springs and spa treatments

▶ Day 3 & 4: Nosara – Yoga retreat and wellness workshops

▶ Day 5 & 6: Puerto Viejo – Caribbean relaxation, beach time, and cultural immersion

▶ Day 7: San José – Final relaxation massage and departure

5. Adventure Sports Extravaganza **(10 DAYS)**

▸ Day 1 & 2: Arenal – Zip lining and waterfall rappelling

▸ Day 3 & 4: Rincón de la Vieja – Volcano hiking and tubing

▸ Day 5 & 6: Monteverde – Bridge walks and ATV tours

▸ Day 7: Manuel Antonio – Parasailing and jet skiing

▸ Day 8 & 9: Dominical – Surfing and stand-up paddleboarding

▸ Day 10: San José – Return and departure

These itineraries are just the beginning of what Costa Rica has to offer. Mix and match activities to suit your interests, or let these ideas inspire a completely unique journey. In Costa Rica, the adventure is yours to create.

Conclusion

Costa Rica, a realm where verdant forests meet azure seas and towering volcanoes stand guard over sprawling valleys, has been the canvas for our exploration in this guide. Through each chapter, we've ventured into the heart of a country that pulsates with life, inviting you to immerse yourself in its natural wonders, engage with its rich culture, and partake in the essence of pura vida.

In Costa Rica, every step is an introduction to the extraordinary: where the rainforest's canopy teems with life, beaches stretch into the horizon, and the air is filled with the calls of exotic birds. This country teaches us the power of nature – not just to awe but to heal, inspire, and unite. Here, the commitment to conservation and sustainability isn't just a policy; it's a way of life, a testament to the respect and love the Costa Ricans have for their land.

Yet, Costa Rica's allure extends beyond its landscapes. It lies in the warmth of its people, the richness of its culture, and the simplicity of life that reminds us of the joy in the everyday. Whether you're savoring a cup of locally grown coffee, dancing to the rhythms of salsa and bachata, or simply sharing stories with locals, you're experiencing the true essence of Costa Rica.

This isn't merely a destination for vacation; it's a place for discovery, learning, and personal growth. Whether your journey involves zip-lining through the cloud forests of Monteverde, soaking in the volcanic hot springs near Arenal, or participating in a turtle conservation project on the Caribbean coast, these experiences forge a deeper connection with the world around us.

Traveling in Costa Rica invites you to embrace flexibility and adventure. The country's unpredictable weather and diverse ecosystems encourage a spirit of adaptability and exploration. It's about making the most of every moment, whether that means finding sunshine amid the rain in the cloud forest or discovering a hidden cove along the Pacific shore.

As visitors, it's crucial to tread lightly, respecting the natural environments and communities that make Costa Rica unique. Follow the principles of eco-tourism by staying on marked trails during hikes, choosing sustainable lodging options, and supporting local businesses. In doing so, you contribute to preserving the beauty and diversity of Costa Rica for future explorers.

To enrich your journey further, consider learning some basic Spanish phrases. Not only is this a sign of respect for the local culture, but it also opens doors to more meaningful interactions. Here are a few phrases to get you started:

▷ "Hola" – Hello

▷ "Gracias" – Thank you

▷ "Por favor" – Please

▷ "¿Cuánto cuesta?" – How much does it cost?

▷ "¿Dónde está el baño?" – Where is the bathroom?

▷ "Me llamo..." – My name is...

▷ "¿Puede ayudarme?" – Can you help me?

- "Un café, por favor" – A coffee, please

- "Buenos días" – Good morning

- "Buenas noches" – Good night

- "No hablo mucho español" – I don't speak much Spanish

- "¿Dónde está...?" – Where is...?

- "Me gustaría..." – I would like...

- "Estoy perdido/a" – I'm lost

In closing, your travels in Costa Rica are a journey into the heart of pura vida, a reminder of the beauty that flourishes when we live in harmony with nature and each other. Here's to the adventures that await, the memories you'll create, and the lessons you'll carry with you long after you've left its shores. Here's to Costa Rica, a country that embodies the spirit of adventure, the richness of culture, and the profound connection to the earth that inspires us all.

In the spirit of Tolkien, "Not all those who wander are lost." Embark on your Costa Rican adventure with an open heart and a curious soul, and let the magic of this country transform you. Pura vida!

Made in United States
North Haven, CT
06 November 2024

59930243R00102